THE KINGDOM OF GOD

Stephen Kaung

ISBN: 978-1-942521-49-5

Available from:

Christian Testimony Ministry
4424 Huguenot Road
Richmond, Virginia 23235

www.christiantestimonyministry.com

Printed in USA

CONTENTS

PREFACE

"For Thine is the kingdom, and the power and the glory, forever." Matthew 6:13 (ASV)

The kingdom of God is one of the most important themes in the whole Bible. It is the message of the Bible and is the message of our Lord Jesus. The kingdom of God was preached by our Lord Himself and continually preached by the apostles. If we know what the kingdom is, we can open the whole Bible, not only the New Testament but the Old Testament—the kingdom is the key.

The Lord's people are called to "seek ye first the kingdom of God", and to pray "let Thy kingdom come,"—a prayer the Lord Himself commands us to pray. It shows that the heart of our Lord is in it—He desires that His kingdom may be manifested upon this earth. The kingdom of the world shall become the kingdom of our Lord and of His Christ. He longs for it; therefore, He asks His church to pray for it. If this is the longing of our Lord, then... **We Must See The Kingdom!**

During the 1986 Christian Family Conference held in Richmond, Virginia, Stephen Kaung shared on the Kingdom of God. These four spoken messages have been transcribed into this book. The spoken form has been preserved and only necessary editing done for clarity.

THINE IS THE KINGDOM

1 Chronicles 29:10-13 And David blessed Jehovah in the sight of all the congregation; and David said, Blessed be thou, Jehovah, the God of our father Israel, for ever and ever. Thine, Jehovah, is the greatness, and the power, and the glory, and the splendour, and the majesty; for all that is in the heavens and on the earth is thine: thine, Jehovah, is the kingdom, and thou art exalted as Head above all; and riches and glory are of thee, and thou rulest over everything; and in thy hand is power and might; and in thy hand it is to make all great and strong. And now, our God, we thank thee, and praise thy glorious name.

Matthew 6:13 And lead us not into temptation, but save us from evil. Authorized Version For thine is the kingdom and the power and the glory forever. Amen.

Shall we pray:

Dear Heavenly Father, we do want to praise and thank Thee for bringing us together here into

Thy presence. We ask, O Lord, that Thou will remove any veil that may be upon any heart that we may behold the glory of the Lord with unveiled face. We do look to Thy Holy Spirit to quicken Thy Word to our hearts and to bring us into Thy truth. We do praise and thank Thee, knowing that Thou art the God who reveals. Grant to us the spirit of wisdom and revelation to the full knowledge of God. We do commit this time into Thy hands, knowing that without Thee, we can do nothing; but with Thee, all things are possible. We are here, Lord; speak; Thy servants hear. We ask in the name of our Lord Jesus. Amen.

The Lord has impressed upon my heart this matter of the kingdom of God. This is the message that John the Baptist preached: "Repent, for the kingdom of the heavens has drawn nigh" (Matthew 3:2). This is the same message that our Lord Jesus taught about the kingdom of God while He was on earth. He said: "The time is fulfilled and the kingdom of the heavens has drawn nigh. Repent and believe in the glad tidings" (Mark 1:15). Our Lord Jesus told us about the spiritual principles of that kingdom in Matthew 5-7. He explained to us the mysteries of the kingdom of the heavens in parables which are found in Matthew 13. He revealed to us the public manifestation of the kingdom that is to come upon this earth in Matthew 24 and 25. He said:

Blessed are the poor in spirit for theirs is the kingdom of the heavens. (Matthew 5:3)

Seek ye first the kingdom of God and His righteousness and all these things shall be added unto you. (Matthew 6:33)

The kingdom of the heavens is taken by violence, and the violent seize on it. (Matthew 11:12)

Fear not, little flock, for it has been the good pleasure of your Father to give you the kingdom. (Luke 12:32)

And these glad tidings of the kingdom shall be preached in the whole habitable earth, for a witness to all the nations, and then shall come the end. (Matthew 24:14)

He testified before Pilate and said:

My kingdom is not of this world; if my kingdom were of this world, my servants had fought that I might not be delivered up to the Jews; but now my kingdom is not from hence. (John 18:36)

After His resurrection, He appeared to His disciples on and off for forty days, and He talked with them about the things of the kingdom of God. So, we find this is the message in the Bible: the kingdom of God.

After the Lord's ascension, on the day of Pentecost, the Holy Spirit came down and the 120 believers were baptized into one body. On that very day, Peter stood up with the eleven, and he preached the kingdom of God to the people. In Acts 2, the whole message is summed up with verses 32, 33, and 36: "God has raised up Jesus and has exalted Him. This Jesus whom you crucified, God has made Him Christ and Lord." It is the message of the kingdom of God.

Later, when Peter went to the house of Cornelius, again he preached to them the kingdom of God. Of course, it was put a little different; to the Gentiles, he said: "This Jesus of whom we are all witnesses, God has ordained Him, God has appointed Him to be the Judge of the living and the dead." That is the message of the kingdom of God.

When Philip went to Samaria, that was his message. He preached to them the kingdom of God and the name of the Lord Jesus (see Acts 8).

The Holy Spirit set apart Paul and Barnabas and they went forward. They went to the lower part of Galatia; and when they returned to these cities, they exhorted the brethren, those who believed in the Lord Jesus, to be steadfast and abide in the faith. They told them that they had to go through many tribulations in order to enter into the kingdom of God. When the Apostle Paul went into the city of Ephesus, he went into the synagogue. There he reasoned with them and persuaded them concerning the kingdom of God. Again, in chapter 20 of the book of Acts, Paul called the elders of the church in Ephesus to come and he said that for the three years he was there, he was teaching them about the kingdom of God.

The book of Acts begins with the kingdom of God. Our Lord Jesus Himself, after He was resurrected, talked to the disciples for forty days. During those forty days, He spoke about nothing but the kingdom of God. Then, the book of Acts ends with the kingdom of God. In chapter 28, while the Apostle Paul was in Rome, though he was a prisoner, he could stay in his own rented apartment. There, he received the people who came to him. He preached to them the kingdom of God, and taught them the things concerning the Lord Jesus.

The kingdom of God is the message of the New Testament. It was preached by the Lord Himself, and continually preached by the apostles. In looking at the writings of the apostles you find this is the same thing that they wrote about throughout the New Testament.

For the kingdom of God is not eating and drinking, but righteousness, and peace, and joy in the Holy Spirit. (Romans 14:17)

For the kingdom of God is not in word, but in power. (1 Corinthians 4:20)

Do ye not know that unrighteous persons shall not inherit the kingdom of God? (1 Corinthians 6:9)

But this I say, brethren, that flesh and blood cannot inherit God's kingdom, nor does corruption inherit incorruptibility. (1 Corinthians 15:50)

In Galatians 5:21, after Paul relates to us the works of the flesh, then he says:

They who do such things shall not inherit God's kingdom.

For this ye are well informed of, knowing that no fornicator, or unclean person, or person of unbridled lust, who is an idolater, has inheritance in the kingdom of the Christ and God. (Ephesians 5:5)

In Colossians 4:11, Paul mentions three fellow workers who are workmen of the kingdom of God: Aristarchus, Justus, and Mark.

In 2 Thessalonians 1:5, Paul mentions how those who believe in the Lord and suffer for the Lord's sake are counted worthy of the kingdom of God.

Now is come the salvation and the power and the kingdom of our God, and the authority of his Christ. (Revelation 12:10)

These are just a few illustrations to show you that the theme of the New Testament is concerned with the kingdom of God.

But do not think that the kingdom of God is just a theme of the New Testament, because as you go back to the Old Testament, you find the same theme. For instance, when the children of Israel came out of Egypt, they crossed the Red Sea; and in Exodus 15, they praised the Lord with a victorious song which ended with a word that Jehovah shall reign forever and ever. That is the kingdom of God.

Then, God brought them to Mount Sinai; and in Exodus 19, God said:He brought them to Himself as on eagle's wings, and if they would keep His covenant and hear His word then God would make them a peculiar people, a people of His own possession among all the nations, and make them a nation of priests. That is God's purpose for His redeemed people.

Thine Jehovah is the kingdom and thou art exalted as head above all. (1 Chronicles 29:11)

For the kingdom is Jehovah's, and he ruleth among the nations. (Psalm 22:28)

And in the days of these kings shall the God of the heavens set up a kingdom which shall not be destroyed; and the sovereignty thereof shall not be left to another people: it shall break in pieces and consume all these kingdoms, but itself shall stand forever. (Daniel 2:44)

And the kingdom shall be Jehovah's. (Obadiah 21)

So, you find that in the Old Testament, the kingdom of God is the theme. As a matter of fact, the kingdom of God is from generation to generation, from ages to ages. Our God is the everlasting God, the eternal God. In Psalm 90, Moses said: "Thou art God from eternity to eternity." God is from eternity to eternity. He is the Sovereign. The kingdom is within Him, and the kingdom began as soon as He started to create the universe.

11

Thy kingdom is a kingdom of all ages, and thy dominion is throughout all generations. (Psalm 145:13)

Jehovah hath established his throne in the heavens, and his kingdom ruleth overall. (Psalm 103:19)

And at the end of the days I Nebuchadnezzar lifted up mine eyes unto the heavens, and mine understanding returned unto me, and I blessed the Most High, and I praised and honoured him that liveth forever, whose dominion is an everlasting dominion, and his kingdom is from generation to generation. (Daniel 4:34)

Brothers and sisters, these few illustrations are to show you that the kingdom of God is one of the most important themes in the whole Bible. To put it another way, the kingdom of God can serve as the key to the whole Bible. If we know what the kingdom of God is, we can open the whole Bible, not only the New Testament, but also the Old Testament.

THE SOVEREIGN OF THE UNIVERSE

What is the kingdom of God? What is kingdom? Those who understand Greek agree that the English translation of the Greek word into kingdom is not very good. Actually, that word in Greek should be translated into English as "the sovereign rule of God". Our God is the Sovereign of the universe, and He rules over all.

When we think of the kingdom, probably, the first thought that comes into our mind is the kingdom as a domain, as a sphere, as a territory over which God rules. Now, that is true. The kingdom of God is a domain; it is a sphere, a territory over which God rules. But if we look at the kingdom in that sense only, we will never be able to understand what the kingdom of God is. If we want to understand what the kingdom of God is, we have to put our emphasis on the Sovereign before we put our emphasis on the rule. In other words, the kingdom of God is the personal rule of God, and the emphasis is on God as the Sovereign of the universe. The Person, the personality, the character, the nature of God

13

governs the domain and characterizes the domain over which He rules.

Let me use an illustration. After our Lord Jesus was raised from the dead, He spent forty days with His disciples, talking to them concerning the things of the kingdom of God. Now you would think after our Lord had risen from the dead and appeared to His disciples, talking to them about the kingdom of God, surely they would have grasped it. But after forty days, our Lord took them to the Mount of Olives; and before He ascended, you know what His disciples asked Him? This was their last chance, and this was something that was going on within them all the time. Their question was: "Lord, is this the time You will restore the kingdom to Israel?" It is true they were concerned with the kingdom, but their very question reveals their concept of the kingdom as a domain, a sphere, a territory. It is geopolitical in nature. Our Lord Jesus answered that question by saying: "It is not for you to know the time or the season." The Lord did not deny that one day the kingdom will be restored to Israel; because, once upon a time, God did take Israel as representative of His kingdom upon the earth; but they lost it. One day in the future, it will be restored, so our Lord did not deny that; but He told them it was not for them to know the time or the season. It means: do not be occupied with that; do not be so focused upon that; the time and the season is not for you to know; it is in the authority of My Father. When My Father sees that the time is right, then He will do it; but you do not know it, and you do not need to know it. Do not be concerned about it. There is something that you need to be concerned about, and that is: you shall receive power.

POWER TO BEAR WITNESS

The Holy Spirit having come upon you, and ye shall be my witnesses both in Jerusalem, and in all Judea and Samaria, and to the end of the earth. (Acts 1:8)

How is the kingdom of God to come? Do not be concerned with the time and the season when the kingdom shall be restored to Israel on earth, but be very much concerned that you will receive power. The Holy Spirit shall come upon you; and when the Spirit of God, when the Holy

15

Spirit shall come upon you, then you will have the power to be My witness.

Lordship of Christ

What is the church to witness of Christ? The church is to witness that Jesus is King, Jesus is Lord. The Lordship of Christ is what the church is to bear witness to. To bear witness is not a matter of just hearing something. In order to bear witness, you need power; and the power comes from the Holy Spirit.

How does the Holy Spirit bring that power to the church? On the day of Pentecost when the Holy Spirit came down upon them, people wondered what it was. Some said they were drunk with new wine, and then Peter and the eleven stood up and said: "No, it is only nine o'clock in the morning, and nobody drinks that early. What you see and hear is that God has raised Jesus up. He has exalted Him, and He has made Him Lord and Christ." The meaning of the baptism with the Holy Spirit is the Lordship of Christ. No one can say "Jesus is Lord" unless he is in the Spirit. It is the Holy Spirit Who reveals Jesus to us; the Lord of all, my Lord. And when the Holy Spirit reveals that to us as individuals and to the church as a corporate body, then individuals and the whole church will submit themselves under the Lordship of Christ. They will hold fast the Head, and then they will be joined together as members of one another. They were no longer 120 individual believers; they became a body of 120 members. "In one Spirit you were baptized into one body."

Oneness of the Body

Dear brothers and sisters, by this very fact, the Lordship of Christ and the oneness of the body, the church becomes that testimony, that witness; and this is powerful. They went out, beginning in Jerusalem, then to all Judea, to Samaria, and to the end of the earth, not only to proclaim that Jesus is Lord, but with their very lives under the Lordship of Christ. They went out as a body; not divided, not scattered, but as a body. Therefore, in the early days, people looked at these believers and said, "Look at these people; how they love one another!" That is the power. The personality of the Lord, Himself, came upon these people, and they became a

17

corporate expression of Christ. That is the kingdom of God.

The kingdom of God is not a geopolitical thing. The kingdom of God is the personal rule of God. It is God, Himself, Christ being formed in His people. His person, His personality is being formed in a corporate body, and there you see the kingdom of God: there He is the Sovereign; there He rules over all; there His authority is obeyed.

HIS KINGDOM ESTABLISHED UPON EARTH

When the people begin to see Jesus as Lord, when they begin to submit themselves to the authority of Christ, and when the character of Christ begins to be formed in this people, you have the domain, you have the sphere, you have the territory. This is the kingdom of God; but before we can have that new order, we have to see Jesus is Lord. If we see Jesus is Lord and accept Him as Lord, then He will raise up a new order upon this earth. That new order will develop and continue until, one day, all powers, authorities, governments, and everything that isopposing to Him will be destroyed; and His kingdom shall be brought upon this earth.

GOD ALL AND IN ALL

First Corinthians 15 is a chapter on resurrection; but in speaking of resurrection, it does bring us to the ultimate, to the very end.

Then the end, when he gives up the kingdom to him who is God and Father; when he shall have annulled all rule and all authority and power. For he must reign until he put all enemies under his feet. The last enemy that is annulled is death. For he has put all things in subjection under his feet. But when he says that all things are put in subjection, it is evident that it is except him who put all things in subjection to him. But when all things shall have been brought into subjection to him, then the Son also himself shall be placed in subjection to him who put all things in subjection to him, that God may be all in all. (1 Corinthians 15:24-28)

Now, we know this is the end. But if we see the end, it tells us the beginning. Even though something had happened, what was in the mind of God, what was purposed by God in the very beginning will all be realized in the end. What do we see in the end? In the end, Christ will annul all powers, all authorities, all rule; and the last to be annulled is death. God will put everything under His feet. He shall rule. When everything is put under His feet, then He will bring everything back into subjection to God that God may be all and in all; and that is the end.

Christ came; He was crucified; He was raised from the dead; He ascended upon high. When He ascended up to heaven, God anointed Him as King (see Psalm 2 or Revelation 5). God has given Him all power in heaven and upon earth; He shall reign, He is reigning. Do you see that He is reigning, now, above, in heaven? He shall reign until He puts all enemies under His feet. We have not seen all the enemies put under His feet yet, but we do see Jesus crowned with glory and honor. He has reigned from His ascension until today; He is still reigning.

Dear brothers and sisters, who is reigning today? Jesus is reigning. He is to subject all things under His feet; God is doing that for Him and to Him. When the last enemy is defeated, death is destroyed. Then all things shall be under His feet, and He will bring the kingdom back to God, that God may be all and in all. This is the kingdom of God.

THINE IS THE KINGDOM

In 1 Chronicles 29, David really understood what the kingdom of God is. David had gathered the people together and shared with them what was in his mind concerning the building of a house for God; but God said that his son, Solomon, would build it. David was shown the pattern for the house of God, and out of his love for God, he prepared gold, silver, and all the things for that house. Then, he encouraged the people to give unto God out of love. How the people responded and gave! When David saw these things, his heart was so warm and touched that he blessed Jehovah in the sight of all the congregation and said:

Blessed be thou, Jehovah, the God of our father Israel, for ever and ever. Thine, Jehovah, is the greatness, and the power, and the glory, and the splendour, and the majesty; for all that is in the

21

heavens and on the earth is thine: thine, Jehovah, is the kingdom. (1 Chronicles 29:10-11)

"Thine is the greatness." The kingdom is great. "Thine is the greatness." Nobody can see the universe that God has created and not acknowledge the greatness of His kingdom. In Psalm 8, when the Psalmist looked up at the heavens and saw the handiwork of God, then he said: "What is man? What is man that God should take care of and be mindful of man?" He saw the greatness of God.

"Thine is the power." In Psalm 104, the Psalmist again saw the power of God. "Thine is the_glory", Psalm 19."Thine is the splendour", Psalm 103."Thine is the majesty", Psalm 105.

As you read the Psalms, you find that the Psalmist and the people know the greatness, the splendour, the glory of the kingdom of God. He said: "You are God, and the kingdom is Yours. You are exalted as Head above all because these are Thy handiwork. Riches and glory are of thee and thou rulest over everything; and in thy hand is power and might; and in thy hand it is to make all great and strong" (1 Chronicles 29:12).

The God Who created the universe is the Lord of the universe. In the beginning, the universe was His kingdom, and we see the greatness and the glory of it. In the prayer that our Lord Jesus taught His disciples to pray in Matthew 6, in the King James Version, you find this: "Thine is the kingdom and the power and the glory forever. Amen." It is the Lord's. The kingdom is the Lord's.

NATURE OF THE KINGDOM

Spiritual Kingdom

What is the nature of this kingdom of God? The kingdom of God is, first of all, spiritual. It does not mean that the kingdom of God is not physical, but basically, the kingdom of God is spiritual in nature. It is because God is Spirit. Therefore, anything that has to do with God has to be basically spiritual. We must worship God in spirit and truth because God is a Spirit.

One day, the Pharisees came to the Lord Jesus and asked Him the question: "When will the kingdom of God come?" The Lord Jesus said: "The kingdom of God does not come by observation. You can not say here or there. The kingdom of God is in the midst of you." Or, some translations say: "It is within you" (see Luke 17:20- 21). Of course, you can either translate it "in the midst of you", or "within you". Strictly speaking, it should be "in the midst of you", because the kingdom of God was not within these Pharisees. What the Lord was trying to tell them was that the kingdom of God is basically spiritual in nature. Do not try to think of it purely as a physical thing: as a realm, a sphere, a territory, a government. It is more than that. It is spiritual in nature. Or, to put it another way: it is in the Spirit. It is by the Spirit that the kingdom of God comes.

The flesh and blood cannot inherit the kingdom of God. The flesh and blood speak of the natural, speak of the physical, but the kingdom of God is for those who are spiritual. One day, Nicodemus came to the Lord and he had this matter of the kingdom of God in his mind. So he said to the Lord Jesus: "You are a teacher, a great teacher coming from heaven." Even though Nicodemus was not able to say it, the Lord knew what was in his heart. Nicodemus was concerned with this matter of the kingdom of God. He thought that he had seen the kingdom of God, but he wanted to enter into that kingdom. He thought that he was just a step short of entering the door of that kingdom, and he needed more teaching, more instruction, or to do something more before he could enter into the kingdom of God. Now that was in his mind, and that was the reason why he came to the Lord Jesus that evening. Before he spoke out, the Lord said: "Unless you are born from above, you do not see the kingdom of God." Nicodemus thought he had seen the kingdom of God, but the Lord said: "You have not; what you saw was not the real thing. Unless you are born from above, unless you are born again, unless you are born of the Spirit, then you will not be able to see the kingdom of God."

Brothers and sisters, will you accept this? If you are not born again, you will not even see the kingdom of God. If you are born of the Spirit, then you can see it, you can enter it; it is yours. It is spiritual in nature.

Kingdom Of Truth

The kingdom of God is a kingdom of the truth. When Pilate was examining our Lord Jesus, he said: "Are You the King of the Jews?" And the Lord said: "Now who says it? I am a King, but My kingdom is not of the world. I come for the truth." And Pilate said: "What is the truth?" But without waiting for the answer from the Lord, he went off; and he never knew the truth (see John 18). Some people are too busy to know the truth. They may ask the question, but they do not wait for the answer.

What is the truth? The Lord said He came to bear witness to the truth. In other words, truth is reality. The whole world is a lie. Do not think that what you see is real; nothing is real. All these are passing away. It is just a big lie; it is false. You see all the people who are living in that lie, believing in that lie, living for that lie; but one day, they will wake up and find it is too late. It passes away. But what is the reality; what is the truth? Christ is the truth. He said: "I am the truth." The Spirit of God is a Spirit of truth; because it is the Spirit of God Who leads us into all truth, Who leads us into all the riches of Christ. That is the kingdom.

If we live in a lie, we are not living in the kingdom of God; but if we live in the truth, in the reality, then we are in the kingdom of God. Of course, truth is not just a teaching, a doctrine. A teaching or a doctrine may be true; but the Lord Jesus said: "Ye shall know the truth and the truth shall set you free" (John 8:32). If any teaching, which is a correct teaching, an orthodox teaching, does not set you free, it is not the truth yet; because the truth shall set you free.

How does the truth come to you? It is by revelation of the Holy Spirit. When the Holy Spirit opens up the Word of God, when He reveals Christ in the Word of God, then it becomes reality to your life and it sets you free. In that sense, you are living, really, in the kingdom of God.

Kingdom Of Love

Who has delivered us from the authority of darkness, and translated us into the kingdom of the Son of His love. (Colossians 1:13)

Once, we were under the authority of the power of darkness. Now, God has delivered us out; and He has translated us into the kingdom of the Son of His love. The kingdom of God is love. "God so loved the world that He gave His only begotten Son." Christ so loved us that He laid down His life for us. The rule of that kingdom is the rule of love.

Oftentimes, we think authority and love are two opposite things. We think if there is authority, then it is so legalistic, so tyrannical, so despotic, and so dictatorial that there is no love in it, there is no feeling to it. We think of love as something that is so gentle, so tender, so indulgent, and so all embracing that there is no sharpness in it at all. But the kingdom which speaks of authority, is the authority of love. There is no authority greater than love. And if any authority is to be exercised, let it be exercised in love; then it will work. Love is the principle of the kingdom of God. That is the reason why the Bible says: "You shall love the Lord your God with all your heart, with all your mind, with all your understanding, with all your soul, with all your strength, and you shall love your neighbor as yourself. These are the greatest of the commandments" (Matthew 22:37,39). The whole commandment of God can be summed up into love, because it is the kingdom of love. God demands that we love Him with all our hearts. I remember one brother said: "The Bible does not say, Love God with your heart. It says, Love God with all your heart." It is not enough just to love God with your heart. Yes, you need to love God with your heart and not your lips; but if it is a divided heart, that is not what God requires. He requires all your heart, all your mind, all your understanding, all your strength; and then to love one another as He has loved us. This is the kingdom of God.

Do we see the kingdom of God today? Do we see the kingdom of God in the church? Do we see the kingdom of God among God's people? Does the world see the kingdom of God in the church? What is our testimony? Where is our testimony? The kingdom of God is the kingdom of love.

Kingdom Of Light

Giving thanks to the Father, who has made us fit for sharing the portion of the saints in light. (Colossians 1:12)

God sent the Apostle Paul to preach the kingdom of God, to deliver the people, to set the captives free, and to bring them from darkness into light that they may have inheritance with the saints in light. The kingdom of God is light because that is the character of God. God is light and there is no darkness in Him.

This is the message.... God is light, and in him is no darkness at all. If we walk in the light as he is in the light, we have fellowship with one another, and the blood of Jesus Christ his Son cleanses us from all sin. (1 John 1:5,7)

Dear brothers and sisters, darkness belongs to the kingdom of Satan. The kingdom of God is the kingdom of light. Now, light here is more than just people studying the Bible and saying: "In my reading, I got a light; I got an understanding. I know how to explain it now." No, this is not what it means. The kingdom of

God is the kingdom of light. It means more than that; because here, the light is none other than God, Himself. He said: "God is light." Of course, His Word is like a lamp that shines upon our path. His Word is light in us; that is true. But in 1 John 1, it says: "God is light." He, Himself, is light; and there is no darkness in Him. He is all transparent. That is the kingdom of God.

One day, when the kingdom of God shall be publicly manifested in the New Jerusalem, the whole city will be full of light. Today, you cannot look at the sun because it is too light, too bright; it will burn your eyes. But during the kingdom age, the sun will be seven times brighter than today. And in eternity, in the holy city, the New Jerusalem, everything will be full of light. The glory of God will fill that city and reflect all over, and all will be transparent. Even the gold will be transparent. You will walk on it, and you will see through it.

Brothers and sisters, are you afraid of that? We want to hide in darkness because there are many things in us that cannot be revealed. Today, if everything that is in your mind is cast on a film, where will you be? But this is the kingdom of God: light. God is light, and how He desires that we walk in the light as He is in the light. It is true that He cannot give us the fulness, His full light to shine upon us, because we cannot stand it. He has to lead us step by step, gradually. But, it is also true that we must walk in the light that God has already shined upon us. If God has revealed His character to you, if He has revealed a little of Himself to you of what He is, His purity, His loveliness, His righteousness, His holiness, and you see your darkness and how the blood of Jesus Christ has cleansed you; and you are walking in the light and having fellowship, then you are walking in the kingdom of God.

Kingdom Of Righteousness

For the kingdom of God is not eating and drinking. (Romans 14:17)

We think of the kingdom of God as eating and drinking. Even when the Lord shall come back one day, in that marriage feast of the Lamb, we think of it as eating and drinking. How our mind is just taken up with all these physical, outward things, instead of seeing the reality of it. And the reality of it is that the kingdom of God is not eating and drinking, nor even in not eating and not drinking. The kingdom of God is in righteousness.

What is righteousness? That is a long word; but to shorten it, it means "right". It means you give God His right. Whenever you give God His right, then you are righteous; you are right in His eyes. He is Sovereign, He is Lord, and He has every right over us. Do you give Him His right? If you give Him His right, you are doing the right thing, and you will be reckoned as righteous. That is the kingdom of God.

Of course, we know that we have no righteousness of our own; and it is because of this we came to the Lord Jesus and received Him as our righteousness. God has made Him our righteousness. We are clothed with Christ, that is true; but after we are clothed with Christ, our righteousness, then the Holy Spirit will work the character of Christ, the righteousness of Christ, into us that we, too, will begin to practice righteousness. Today, even though God's people have received Christ as their righteousness, oftentimes, they do not live righteously. And the opposite of righteousness is sin, because sin is taking away the right of God. How we need in our practical, daily living to be righteous because this is His character; and if we are righteous, then we are in the kingdom of God.

THE KINGDOM MANIFESTED

What is the kingdom of God? The kingdom of God is the personal rule of God. Are you under His personal rule? Each one of us is responsible for this. It is open to us; we can enter in. If we accept the Lordship of Christ, let Him be Lord in our lives, and, corporately, accept Him as the Head over the whole body, then the kingdom of God is manifested. David said: "Thine Jehovah is the kingdom."

Brothers and sisters, can we say that? Can we, with honesty, say, "Thine is the kingdom"? The kingdom belongs to Thee and the power, because Thy power is able to bring that kingdom into us and upon the whole earth. And the glory belongs to Thee, because everything will end up in glory to God. Let us be before the Lord during these days and have before us the kingdom of

God, the personal rule of Christ, and let us submit ourselves to Him and let His kingdom come on earth as it is in heaven.

Shall we pray:

Dear Heavenly Father, unless Thou dost reveal Thy kingdom to us, we may talk about it, we may read about it, we may think about it, we may think that we know it, and yet we do not see it; we are not living in it. So our Father, we just pray that during these days, Thou wilt grant us the spirit of wisdom and revelation that we may see Thy kingdom, that it is not something external, something physical only, something that is just an external government. But Lord, we ask that Thou will show us that the kingdom of God is inward, within us, real, spiritual. It demands that we love, we walk in the light, and we be righteous. Lord, we do pray that we will not be careless, that we may really look to Thee to so show us Thy kingdom, and bring us into Thy kingdom, abundantly, through Thy Holy Spirit. We commit ourselves to Thee, and to Thee be the glory. In the name of our Lord Jesus. Amen.

THE HEAVENS DO RULE

Daniel 4:19-27 Then Daniel, whose name is Belteshazzar, was astonied for one hour, and his thoughts troubled him. The king spoke and said, Belteshazzar, let not the dream, nor its interpretation, trouble thee. Belteshazzar answered and said, My lord, the dream be to them that hate thee, and its interpretation to thine enemies! The tree that thou sawest, which grew and was strong, whose height reached unto the heavens, and the sight of it to all the earth; whose leaves were beautiful, and its fruit abundant, and in it was food for all; under which the beasts of the field dwelt, and in whose branches the birds of the heavens had their habitation: it is thou, O king, who art grown and become strong; for thy greatness is grown, and reacheth unto the heavens, and thy dominion to the end of the earth. And whereas the king saw a watcher and a holy one coming down from the heavens, and saying, Hew the tree down, and destroy it; nevertheless leave the stump of its roots in the earth, even with a band of iron and brass, in the tender grass of the field; and let it be bathed with the dew of heaven, and let his portion be with the beasts of the field, till seven times pass over him:this is the interpretation, O king, and it is the decree of the Most High, which cometh upon my lord the king: They shall drive thee from men, and thy dwelling shall be with the beasts of the field, and they shall make thee to eat grass as oxen, and thou shalt be bathed with the dew of heaven; and seven times shall pass over thee, till thou know that the Most High ruleth over the kingdom of men, and giveth it to whomsoever he will. And whereas it was commanded to leave the stump of the roots of the tree; thy kingdom shall remain unto thee, after that thou shalt know that the heavens do rule. Therefore, O king, let my counsel be acceptable unto thee, and break off thy sins by righteousness, and thine iniquities by shewing mercy to the poor; if it may be a lengthening of thy tranquility.

Daniel 4:34-35 And at the end of the days I Nebuchadnezzar lifted up mine eyes unto the heavens, and mine understanding returned unto me, and I blessed the Most High, and I praised and honoured him that liveth forever, whose dominion is an everlasting dominion, and his kingdom is from generation to generation. And all the inhabitants of the earth are reputed as nothing; and he doeth according to his will in the army of the heavens, and among the inhabitants of the earth; and none can stay his hand, or say unto him, What doest thou?

Shall we pray:

Dear Heavenly Father, we are in Thy presence, and we do ask Thee to speak to us through Thy Word that we may hear Thy voice, that we may see Thy vision, that we may be led into Thy truth, that we may be able to stand with Thee for Thy purpose to be fulfilled on earth as it is in heaven. We commit this time into Thy hands, and we trust Thee. In the name of our Lord Jesus. Amen.

The kingdom of God is the personal rule of God. It is the corporate expression of God, Himself. Therefore, the emphasis should be on God: His character, His person, His personality. He imprints His own image upon a domain, upon a people; and that domain is called the kingdom of God, and that people are the people of the kingdom.

Now, we would like to go a step further and see how "The heavens do rule". We find this phrase, "The heavens do rule", in the book of Daniel. In order to understand this, we need to go into the history of the kingdom of God. We have already mentioned that the very concept of the kingdom of God is in God, Himself. The beginning of the history of the kingdom of God was when God began to create the universe. In the beginning, God created the heavens and the earth with a view of the kingdom in His heart. He began to create the universe so that it might become His kingdom, might become an expression of Himself, and be under His rule.

THE CHARACTER OF GOD EXPRESSED IN THE UNIVERSE

In Colossians 1:16, it says that our Lord Jesus is the image of the invisible God, the first born of all creation, for by Him all things were created. From the original, we know that the word by is not correct, although later on you do find it there. "All things are created by Him, through Him and unto Him." In the original, "All things were created by Him" is "All things were created in Him." When the translators translated the Bible, they could not figure out how all things could be created in Him. So, the only way they could put it into English was to put "by Him". It is easier for us to understand that all things were created by Him than to understand that all things were created in Him. What does it mean? When He created all these things, not only did these things come out of His mind; He designed them; but He designed them according to what He is.

For instance, an architect will design a building. The building is not in existence yet, but that building is already in the architect's mind. In his mind he sees that building. If the architect is very artistic, then the building he designs is very beautiful. Or if the architect is very practical, then the building he designs will be an efficient building. So, when you look at the building, you can see, really, the character of the architect. It is his expression. He put his own character upon that which he designed. Therefore, we may say that the building is built in him. After it is built in him, after he designs it, then the general contractor can build it; it is built by him. After it is finished, it is given to the owner to be for him.

When God created all things, He created all things in Christ, His Son. His Son designed everything, and He designed it according to what He is, His character and His nature. He cannot design anything ugly; He cannot design anything impure; He cannot design anything shameful; because He is holy, He is pure, He is beautiful. On all things that God created, you see the imprint of His hand, of His character. The Psalmist said: "The heavens declare the glory of God and the firmament showeth His handiwork" (Psalm 19:1). When God created all things, He not only created them by His power, but we also see His nature, His character in all things. When the universe came out of the mind and of the hands of God, that universe is the kingdom of God; because the whole universe is a corporate expression of who He is, what He is; and He rules over all. He rules over the universe according to His own character. The universe came out to express His character, and He rules over the universe according to what He is, His character.

THE FIRST WORLD

How beautiful, how glorious, how blessed the first world must have been! We just cannot imagine. There, God was on the throne. There, His authority was unchallenged and accepted by all that He had created. There, the angelic beings worshipped God with their whole hearts, and they served God with willingness. There, all the created beings lived together in peace and harmony. There, even the inanimate things, the hills, the trees, all these things, spoke of the glory of God. The whole universe was a great harmony, and God ruled over all according to His nature. What a blessed condition, what a blessed state it must have been.

In Hebrews 1, it says: "God has established His Son to be the heir of all things, by whom the world was created" (v. 2). The word world, actually, is a Hebrew term, and it means "the universe". The universe was created by the Son of God, and God established Him as the heir of all things. Or to put it another way: before God created all things, God's will was to make His Son to be the heir of all things. After all things were created, God said: It is all Yours; it is Yours. He inherited all things. God appointed Him as the King over the universe, and the Lord Jesus, the King, the Son of God will rule over the whole universe with the very character of God. What a blessed state it must be.

THE REBELLION

The kingdom of God began in that blessed state. We know a little bit of the blessedness of it because when we go to 1 Corinthians 15, there we find the end. In chapter 15:24, it says: "Then the end...." When the end comes, then the Son will subject all things to the Father, that God may be all and in all. So in the end, that blessed state will again appear; and by the end, we can understand the beginning of the kingdom of God. We do not know how long that blessed condition continued, but at one point of time, something happened; we know there was a rebellion. We believe Isaiah 14 refers to the rebellion that happened in the universe even before man was created. In chapter 13, Isaiah was prophesying about Babylon, "the burden of Babylon". But then he began to prophesy something that you just cannot apply to Babylon. These words in Isaiah 14:12-15 cannot be applied to any human being. So, people believe that we have a hint of what happened in the universe when the harmony of the universe was broken.

How art thou fallen from heaven, Lucifer, son of the morning! Thou art cut down to the ground, that didst prostrate the nations! (Isaiah 14:12)

Lucifer means brilliant star, "son of the morning". The understanding is that when God first created the universe, the first beings that He created were the angels, angelic beings, spirits. Some people think that, probably, Lucifer, being the son of the morning, was the first created being. Lucifer was an archangel, and God created him in such beauty and endowed him with such power. But somehow, this Lucifer, the son of the morning, began to think of himself.

And thou didst say in thy heart, I will ascend into the heavens, I will exalt my throne above the stars of God, and I will sit upon the mount of assembly, in the recesses of the north; I will ascend above the heights of the clouds, I will be like the Most High. (v. 13)

We remember that in the kingdom of God, God is all and in all. Originally, nobody thought of himself; there was no self- consciousness. All the attention was upon God. Everything was for God; everything was for His glory. God was all and in all. But somehow, this Lucifer, the son of the morning, began to think of himself. He began to be self-conscious; he began to be interested in himself; he began to be self-centered. He said: "I, I, I. I will ascend into the heavens. I will exalt my throne above the stars of God. I will sit upon the mountain of assembly in the recesses of the north."Some people believe that is where the throne of God is set. He wanted to be in the privy council of God. In the Godhead, there is a council: God the Father, God the Son, and God the Holy Spirit. And this created being wanted to be a part in that council in the Godhead."I will ascend above the heights of the cloud. I will be like the Most High."In other words, he was not contented with what he was, as created by God. He was not satisfied with where God had put him. He wanted something more than God had ordained for him. He was not willing to be under God, he wanted to be equal with God; and because of this, he was cast out of the heavens.

In Ezekiel 28, we learn a little more about Lucifer, the archangel. Again, people believe this applies to the archangel, because you cannot apply it to any human being. The prophet, Ezekiel, was prophesying in verse 2, concerning the prince of Tyre; and then, from the prince of Tyre, he began to prophesy about the king of Tyre. People believe that the prince of Tyre actually refers to Tyre, the ruler of Tyre. But from that, he projects to the king of Tyre, which cannot be applied to any human being. So the prophecy goes beyond the Tyre on earth, and reaches back to the beginning.

Son of man, take up a lamentation upon the king of Tyre, and say unto him, Thus saith the Lord Jehovah: Thou, who sealest up the measure of perfection, full of wisdom and perfect in beauty, thou wast in Eden, the garden of God. (Ezekiel 28:12)

He was created as the measure of perfection. So far as the created being is concerned, he was the standard of perfection. He was full of wisdom and perfect in beauty. He was in Eden, the garden of God, not the Eden upon the earth.

47

Every precious stone was thy covering: the sardius, the topaz, and the diamond, the chrysolite, the onyx, and the jasper, the sapphire, the carbuncle, and the emerald, and gold. The workmanship of thy tambours and of thy pipes was in thee. (v. 13)

He was gifted with music, and God gave him all this musical talent in order that he may praise God, that he may lead the singing and worship unto God.

In the day that thou wast created were they prepared. Thou wast the anointed covering cherub. (v. 14)

The tabernacle of Moses was built according to the pattern God gave him on the Mount. In that tabernacle, in the holiest of all, there was the ark with the mercy seat; and the glory of God sat upon that mercy seat. Over the ark, there were two cherubim, and these two cherubim were the covering. They were like the arms or the back of that throne. Lucifer, this archangel was actually one of the anointed, covering cherubim.

And I had set thee so: thou wast upon the holy mountain of God; thou didst walk up and down in the midst of stones of fire. Thou wast perfect in thy ways, from the day that thou wast created. (v. 15)

When God created that angel, he was perfect. We do not know how long he remained in that perfect way "till unrighteousness was found in thee". We have already said righteousness is giving God His right. Even though he was the first created being, even though he was the measure of perfection, yet he was still created by God; and being created by God, he should give God His right. He should worship God, he should depend upon God, he should look up to God, that is giving God His right. But here it says: "Till unrighteousness was found in thee". Unrighteousness simply means you deprive God of His rights. You take His right away and try to apply it to yourself, that is unrighteousness.

By the abundance of thy traffic they filled the midst of thee with violence, and thou hast sinned. (v. 16)

God had entrusted him with much, God had given him many talents; but he began to abuse the authority and the gifts that God had given to him. He tried to draw everything unto himself, and there was violence. He tried to push his way upon other angels and upon that which God had put under his rule. He did not rule according to God, but according to himself and what he could get; and he sinned.

Therefore have I cast thee as profane from the mountain of God, and have destroyed thee, O covering cherub, from the midst of the stones of fire. Thy heart was lifted up because of thy beauty; thou hast corrupted thy wisdom by reason of thy brightness. (v. 17)

Pride came into his heart. He was so clever, and that corrupted him. Because of that, the Lord said: "I have cast thee to the ground." God cast him out.

In the beginning, the universe that God created was perfect, harmonious, peaceful; it was under the loving care and rule of Christ, God's Son; it was so blessed. But the trouble began when that archangel began to think of himself and tried to grasp for himself. He began to manifest a character that was contradictory to the character of God. He began to exhibit a kind of character that was different from the character of the kingdom of God. Even before he was cast out, he was already manifesting an opposing character that did not belong to the kingdom of God. In the kingdom of God, God is all and in all; God's authority is respected. God is selfless; but this character was full of self: "I, I, I." Everything was just for himself, and because of this he could not remain in the kingdom of God. That is the reason why he was cast out, because God said: Now, you do not belong here. Unfortunately, he had influenced a third of the angelic beings to follow him; there was a rebellion among the angelic beings. After he was cast out, that was the beginning of Satan. He made himself Satan, the adversary of God; and he tried to set up his own kingdom in opposition to the kingdom of God. The kingdom of God is characterized by love, but the kingdom of Satan is characterized by hate. Everything was opposite to God. He tried to set up his kingdom upon the earth, because most likely, our planet was under the dominion of that archangel in the beginning. So that is why, when he fell down, the whole planet entered into corruption and emptiness.

Brothers and sisters, here, we need to understand two things: the kingdom of God has a broad sense, and it has a narrow, strict sense. In the broad sense of the kingdom of God, the sovereign rule of God, He rules over all things that He has created. He created all, and He rules over all, rebellious or obedient. Just because there was rebellion, it does not mean that those who rebelled are no longer under the authority of God; God's authority is still over them. They could not escape the government of God. Do not think that when there is rebellion you get out of God's government or out from under His authority; you cannot. You are still under His authority. In the broad sense, He rules over all, obedient or rebellious.

But in the strict sense, in the real sense, in the narrow sense, in the sense that God intends His kingdom to be, the kingdom of God is over those who obey Him, those who submit to His authority, those who allow Him to work out His own character in their lives. Over these people, you see the real kingdom of God. We have to understand that the kingdom of God has these two different senses. Because Lucifer rebelled against God does not mean he escaped God's government. God cast him out. God's government, God's judgment was upon him, and has been upon him ever since. God might use him; but one day, God will finish him. So, he did not really escape the rule of God. In one sense, he was not in the kingdom of God because he exhibited a different character; but in another sense, God's kingdom is still over him.

However, God did not give up His original purpose. He wanted a kingdom, His kingdom. He wanted creation to be His kingdom, to manifest His glory, to submit to His rule; and that will be blessed. So, He began to work; and that is where man came into the picture. In Genesis 1, you find that God used six days to repair the world, to make it habitable; and on the sixth day, He created man.

GOD'S PURPOSE FOR MAN

Brothers and sisters, why did God create man? What was behind the creation of man? What does God want man for? Again, it is with the kingdom in view. God created man according to His image, after His likeness; and after He created them, He gave them dominion over the fowls of the air, the creatures of the land, and even the fish of the sea. God said: "Multiply and subdue the earth." God created man in His own image, giving him the potential, the possibility, the capacity to receive the very life of God into himself. By that very life, he will be able to exercise dominion, to subdue all things, to bring everything that was in a state of rebellion, in a state of corruption, in a state of vanity into subjection unto God that God may be all and in all, that His kingdom may be restored. That is why man was created.

Man was not created for himself. We are not created to enjoy God's created things. Of course, He does want us to enjoy them; but God created us with a purpose. God said: "I am going to create man a little lower than the angels." There is no glory to God for Him to just blow upon the rebellious angel and finish him. But God, in His wisdom, created man a little inferior to the angels. So far as the order of creation is concerned, angelic beings are higher than man. Their intellect, and everything is higher than man, and we are a little inferior. God created the universe so big, so glorious; yet, as the Psalmist said: "What is man that thou art mindful of him? and the Son of man that thou visiteth him? Thou hast made him a little lower than the angels, and hast crowned him with glory and honor,... thou has put all things under his feet" (Psalm 8:4-6). This is the reason why God created man, you and me.

Brother Sparks said: "Man is the custodian of the great purpose of God." Think of that. Do not think too little of yourself. So far as God's creating you is concerned, He has entrusted the recovery of His kingdom into your hands. God said: "Even though you are a little lower than the angels, I want you to take care of My kingdom." But the kingdom of God is not just physical; it is not something that God can build by decree. "Now, I want a kingdom, and that is it, whether you cooperate or not." Strictly speaking, that is not the kingdom that God wants. God wants a kingdom that will be a reflection of Himself, and that is the reason why we have a moral responsibility. God created us with a free will; He does not want to force us. As a matter of fact, God gives us a free will to choose. God says: "I have created you. This is what I want you to be and what I want you to do, but I will not force you to do it. I will let you choose whether you will obey Me or you will disobey Me."

MAN'S FAILURE

God put two trees in the garden: the tree of life, and the tree of the knowledge of good and evil. God said to man: "All the trees in the garden you can freely eat, and that includes the tree of life; but the tree of the knowledge of good and evil you shall not eat; on the day that you eat thereof you shall surely die" (see Genesis 2:16-17). Why did God do such a thing? Sometimes, we think that if God had not put that tree in the garden it would have saved lots of trouble; not only for us, but also for God. Or sometimes, people think, "Well, it is just eating a fruit, and

God punished man so severely that it does not seem to be too just." But what is the principle behind it? God created man according to His image and gave him dominion over the birds, over the beasts, over the fishes. But God said: "You are above all the created things, but you are below Me. You have to learn to obey, and your blessing is in obeying Me. You are fulfilling your destiny when you obey Me." It is a tremendous thing. Whether we will give God His right; whether we begin to be selfish and think only of ourselves; whether pride comes into us that we want to be like God, we may choose. So, God put man in that garden and said: "This tree you shall not eat. It is not good for you because you shall surely die." We do not know how long man obeyed God, but unfortunately, man betrayed God's trust. God put such trust upon man, yet man betrayed Him. Yes, man was tempted; but man made the choice. And it is the same story: "It is good for me; I will be wise; I will be like God; I do not need God anymore; I am God myself." This is the principle of sin. Man fell into sin; and he handed over to God's enemy, not only himself, but the dominion over the earth. So,

Satan became the prince of this world, the ruler of this earth. What a tragedy!

GOD'S CONTINUED SEARCH FOR A REPRESENTATIVE

But God did not give up; He continued to work. He began with one man: Abel. Then, He found Enoch; He found Noah; He found Abraham. From one person, He continued on to a family; from one family, He went to tribes; from tribes, He went to a nation. God began to work, and He chose one nation out of all the nations to be a representation of the kingdom of God. Even though it was temporary and partial, yet the nation of Israel was chosen by God out of all the nations to be His kingdom upon the earth. If you read the history of the nation of Israel from God's standpoint, you find that God set them apart from all the nations. When God delivered them out of Egypt and they passed through the Red Sea, they sang the song of victory and they ended that song of victory by saying that Jehovah reigns for ever and ever.

In Exodus 19, God brought them to Mount Sinai and said: "Now I have brought you to

Myself. If you keep My commandments and My covenant, then I will make you a people of My own possession out of all the nations. You shall become a kingdom of priests." The nation of Israel had become a theocracy; it was under the sovereign rule of God. All of the other nations had their own kings; but the nation of Israel did not have a king, because God was their King. They were under the sovereign rule of God. And because they were under the sovereign rule of God, they lived in a land flowing with milk and honey, with brooks and waterfalls, a land with wheat and barley, a land with iron and brass. God was looking after them and ruling over them according to what He is. They were blessed. They became the first nation among all nations. The oracles of God were given to them. The covenant of God was with them. David and Solomon became kings, but they were representing God. God was their King. That was the nation of Israel.

Israel was not just a nation chosen as the kingdom of God that God may rule over them and be all unto them; but through them, God was going to demonstrate to the whole world what the kingdom of God is like. Through the nation of Israel, the Word of God was to go forth until the whole world was brought in subjection unto God. Israel had a mission; but unfortunately, it failed. The controversy of God with Israel is over one matter: abomination, idol worshipping. Instead of submitting to the rule of God, they began to worship idols, they began to put their loyalty to another rule; and even though God sent prophet after prophet to warn them and to woo them, they would not listen. Finally, God said: I have to set it aside, temporarily.

THE LAST ADAM

But thank God, the second Man, the last Adam, came. Two thousand years ago, God sent His beloved Son into the world to be a Man; and what a Man! In that Man is the kingdom of God. He not only preached the kingdom of God, He is the kingdom of God; because in that Man, God is all and in all. The authority of God is never challenged. The one thing that concerns Him is the Father's will. If it was the Father's will for Him to go to the cross, to the cross He went. In the life of our Lord Jesus, the kingdom of God is fully manifested, not temporarily, nor partially, but the very character of God is fully manifested in this Man: the spiritual nature, the truth, the love, the light, the righteousness. He is the kingdom of God. He not only lived as the kingdom of God, but on the cross, He defeated the enemy; He defeated that kingdom of darkness. He spoiled principalities and authorities that were in rebellion against God, and He made a public show of them by the cross. Personally, He is the kingdom of God; and by living out the kingdom principles, He destroyed the kingdom of darkness.

In His resurrection, He gave birth to a corporate body, the church. The church is the extension of Christ. He is the Head; the church is the body. The church is where He expresses Himself, corporately. He began to gather people unto Himself; He worked upon these people until they began to manifest the character of God, the character of Christ, and until they submitted themselves to the Lordship of Christ completely, with no questioning and no challenging. The kingdom of God is now among a people, and through the church, God is going to bring back

His kingdom to the universe in full manifestation.

DANIEL, THE GOVERNMENT OF GOD

Now, let's go back to Daniel. The very name, Daniel, means "God is judge", "the government of God". When Daniel was a teenager, he was taken into Babylonian captivity as a hostage. The nation of Israel was on the verge of destruction. The government of the world began to move away from the hand of the nation of Israel into the hands of the Gentiles. God's people were in captivity. Very soon, Jerusalem would be destroyed; the temple would be destroyed. Through the seventy years of captivity, God was never addressed as the God of the heavens and of the earth. God was addressed as the God of the heavens, as if He had retreated into heaven and had lost the earth. He had no testimony upon the earth because His people, the people of His testimony, were in captivity. Jerusalem, the place where He had put His name, was destroyed, and the temple where He dwelt was destroyed. Of course, He left the temple before it was destroyed. There was no testimony of the kingdom of God upon the earth.

Daniel In Captivity

Daniel was a captive of the Gentiles, who were in control in government. By all outward appearance, the kingdom of God did not rule; man ruled. But in the life of Daniel, in the very personal life of Daniel, you see the kingdom of God. He was not only a prophet of the kingdom, of the government of God; but, as a person, he was, literally, under the sovereign rule of God, the personal rule of God.

The king, Nebuchadnezzar, wanted to choose young men who had been taken captive from all the different nations, men who were the best, the most clever, the most handsome, with the most potential, and train them for three years in order that they may stand in his court and serve him. Daniel had no choice; he was a hostage, and he was chosen to be one of these people. Instead of being trained to serve God, he was now being trained to serve Nebuchadnezzar, the Gentile king.

Daniel's Obedience To God

During those three years they were given the royal food and the royal wine in order to educate them, in order to nourish them, and to prepare them for standing before the emperor. The world knew how to choose the best, and they demanded the best. Nevertheless, this young man, who was maybe eighteen or so, purposed in his heart not to defile himself. We are told this royal food was offered, first, to idols and then was given to these young people. So, Daniel purposed in his heart not to be defiled by idols, but to keep himself pure for God, whom he would serve. It was very difficult, because he had no choice. He asked for permission to try out with just water and plain food, and God honored that. God gave him and his three companions great wisdom, especially in judicial things. Daniel had visions, and he interpreted dreams and visions. Daniel kept himself pure for God, under the rule of heaven. When he began to be manifested in the royal court, Nebuchadnezzar said, "Now you can interpret, you know the interpretations", and he said, "No, God reveals it to you. It is not me; it is God." He had humility.

Daniel's Faith In God

Daniel had great faith; he believed in God. Three times a day, he opened his window and prayed toward Jerusalem, even though the royal decree was that no one could ask anything from anyone or any god during a month; and if he did, he would be thrown into the lions' den. But Daniel prayed; he had faith. Here was a man under the rule of heaven; and because, in a sense, he was the embodiment of the kingdom of God, he was able to point out to the Gentile king that "The heavens do rule".

Dear brothers and sisters, if we want to tell the world that "The heavens do rule", first of all, we have to know if heaven rules over us. If heaven does not rule over us, we have no right; and even if we try to proclaim it, there will be no power. But Daniel lived under the rule of heaven. Even though he lived under the most difficult situations, yet he lived under the rule of heaven. Then, God used that vessel to tell the world. So far as the world was concerned, God had been dismissed to heaven; man was in control now. But God, through Daniel, told the world this was not true; the heavens still rule.

Nebuchadnezzar's Vision

Nebuchadnezzar dreamed a dream. He saw an image, a huge man with a golden head and all these things. Nobody knew the dream, and nobody could interpret it. So, Daniel and his friends prayed to God and God gave him the interpretation; and he told Nebuchadnezzar. God revealed His thought concerning the future, the time of the Gentiles. The government is now in the hands of the Gentiles; it began with Nebuchadnezzar. "You are the golden head, and there will be silver and so forth; but finally, there will be a stone cut out without hands. This stone will smash the whole image, they will disappear, and that stone will grow and fill the universe." That is the kingdom of God. Nebuchadnezzar was pleased with the interpretation, but he did not learn the lesson. In other words, God was telling him: "Do not think that you rule. I give you a time to rule that is true; but one day, My kingdom shall be established." That should have humbled him; but instead of being humbled, he got proud and made a huge image all of gold. It was all himself, and not even the Medes or Persians or Greeks or Romans. He was everything, and he asked everybody to bow down when the music rang. The result was that the three friends of Daniel, who were under the rule of heaven, said: "We will not. There is no need to talk about it; we will not bow down. God will deliver us. Even if God does not deliver us, we will not bow." God delivered them, and Nebuchadnezzar had to acknowledge that God overruled him.

But he still did not understand, so God gave him another vision, another dream. In Daniel 4, he saw that tree cut off, the decree of heaven. Daniel explained to him what it meant and asked him to humble himself, but he would not. Daniel told him: "The heavens do rule. Do not think that you rule; the heavens do rule. "But he refused to repent, and he became insane for seven years. When he woke up, he lifted up his eyes to heaven and acknowledged that the kingdom of God is an everlasting kingdom. "The heavens do rule." The whole book of Daniel is telling us that no matter what you see, God still rules over all.

STANDING WITH GOD FOR HIS PURPOSE

Brothers and sisters, here we need to learn two things. First, we need to be in the real kingdom of God. We need to be under the Lordship of Christ that God may manifest Himself through us to fulfill His purpose for the church to bring in His kingdom.

Second, today, we live in a hostile world. The ruler of this world is the enemy of God, and he tries in every way to press us down and deviate our course. He tries every way to destroy us and get us out of God's kingdom; because he knows that if the kingdom of God is fulfilled in us, then his kingdom is finished. So he tries to finish us up to prolong his days. Oftentimes, we feel the pressure of the world. Oftentimes, we feel the oppression, and everything pressing us that we will compromise, we will give up, we will give in. "Well, it is no use; who are we?"

Brothers and sisters, at this time, let us remember one thing: "The heavens do rule". God is still on the throne. He is still ruling over the kingdom of man, and we need to stand with Him. We will not accept the status quo. We will stand with Him, and declare that "The heavens do rule". And if we stand with Him, the heavens will bear upon the earth and bring in the purpose of God.

Shall we pray:

Dear Heavenly Father, we worship Thee. Thou hast created us for that tremendous purpose of subduing all things to be under Thy feet. But Lord, we have betrayed Thee. We thank Thee that Thou does not give us up. Thou didst send Thy beloved Son into the world to deliver us out of the power of darkness into the kingdom of the Son of Thy love. Oh Father, what can we do but to submit ourselves to the Lordship of Christ? Lord, we want Thy kingdom to come upon us and through us, into this world. We ask Thee, Lord, that by Thy grace, we may stand with Thee and declare, as Daniel did: "The heavens do rule." Oh, how we thank Thee. In the name of our Lord Jesus. Amen.

THY KINGDOM COME

Matthew 6:9-13 Thus therefore pray ye:Our Father who art in the heavens, let thy name be sanctified, let thy kingdom come, let thy will be done as in heaven so upon the earth; give us today our needed bread, and forgive us our debts, as we also forgive our debtors, and lead us not into temptation, but save us from evil. King James Version For thine is the kingdom and the power and the glory forever. Amen.

Shall we pray:

Dear Heavenly Father, we do praise and thank Thee that Thou has gathered us together unto the name of Thy beloved Son, our Lord Jesus Christ. We do thank Thee for Thy precious promise: "Where two or three are gathered together unto My name, there am I in the midst of them." So Lord, we just believe that Thou art here in our midst, and our prayer is that Thou will grant a spirit of wisdom and revelation that we may see Thee: we may see Thee, we may hear Thee, and we may be transformed and be conformed to Thy image. Lord, we just trust Thy Holy Spirit to move among Thy people and finish Thy new creation. We ask in Thy precious name. Amen.

The kingdom of God belongs to God. He has put His imprint upon the domain over which He rules; and He does rule over all, even though there has been rebellion among the angelic beings and man. The heavens do rule over the kingdom of man.

Now we would like to consider this matter of "Thy kingdom come." We are all familiar with this prayer. We call it the Lord's Prayer. Some say, "It is not the Lord's Prayer; it is the prayer that our Lord Jesus teaches His disciples to pray. So, it is the church's prayer."Now, personally, I believe that our Lord Jesus will never teach anything that He does not do Himself. It is true, this is a prayer that our Lord Jesus teaches His church to pray; but, certainly, this is the prayer of our Lord Jesus, Himself, and He asks us to join with Him in this prayer.

THE NAME

"Our Father, who art in heaven, let Thy name be sanctified; hallowed be Thy name." What is the name? "Our Father, who art in heaven." How do we sanctify that name? How do we honor that name? The best way to honor or the real way to sanctify that name is to hold on to that name, to be named under that name, to be put under the authority of that name, and let the character of our Father in heaven characterize us. In the so-called Sermon on the Mount, it is said:

Be ye therefore perfect as your heavenly Father is perfect. (Matthew 5:48)

The best way to honor the name of the Father, to sanctify the name of our Father in heaven is to be like Him: like Father, like Son. The best way to sanctify the Father is to let His heavenly character be our character.

Sometimes, we think the Lord's Prayer, or the prayer of the church, is concerned with something that is in the future. One day in the future, the name of God, the Father, will be hallowed and sanctified. Now that is true;

because, one day, every knee shall bow and every tongue confess that Jesus is Lord; and when that day comes, certainly, the name of God will be sanctified. However, if you read the context, the Lord's Prayer, or the prayer of the church, is not just concerned with the future; it is concerned with now. Matthew, chapters 5, 6, and 7, the so- called Sermon on the Mount, deal with the spiritual reality and spiritual principles of the kingdom of God. And when we come into this matter of spiritual principles and realities, we are no longer bound by time or space. It is timeless; it is spaceless; it is eternal; it is forever. Therefore, this prayer is also timeless. We cannot just dismiss this prayer to the future, that is to say: "One day this will happen; it is an expectation, anticipation of some future date." Now, that is true; there is that expectation there, there is anticipation of the full realization of all God's purpose. But let us remember that this prayer begins today: "Let Thy name be hallowed." It is not only in the future, but even now, here on this earth.

THY WILL BE DONE ON EARTH

"Thy will be done on earth as it is in heaven." The will of God is done in heaven by the angelic hosts; but the will of God must also be done on earth as it is in heaven. Who will do the will of God on earth? the saints, the Christians, the believers, the church. In heaven we find that God's will is being done. There is no question about it. The angelic host carries out the will of God, executes the will of God as God wills it to be; but the problem, now, is on earth. The will of God is supposed to be done by the saints, to be executed by the church; but has the church executed the will of God on earth? Are we doing the will of God on earth as it is done in heaven? This is our prayer. It is not for a future day; although, one day, His will will be done in the whole universe. All His plans, all His counsels will be fully realized; that is true. But we have to remember that in this prayer, we are praying not just for the future, we are praying that now His will will be done on earth, in us, as it is in heaven.

THY KINGDOM COME TODAY

In between these two petitions is "Thy kingdom come." I have to confess that when I prayed, "Thy kingdom come", I was thinking of the future; that I should pray that, one day, God will bring His kingdom upon this earth: "Thy kingdom come." It is not here yet, but I want to pray that it will come on earth, one day. I wonder if this is your concept. When you are praying, "Thy kingdom come", how do you feel? Are you just looking forward to the future? Or do you have the sense that, as you pray, "Thy kingdom come", it is to come now, it is to come to your life, it is to be a reality, even today? If "Thy name be sanctified" is for today; if "Thy will be done on earth as it is in heaven" is for today; then, "Thy kingdom come" is, also, for today. As we pray, we want to see the kingdom of God come upon us to be a reality in our midst, even here and now.

GOD'S NAME, GOD'S KINGDOM, GOD'S WILL

Name speaks of the Person: God, our Lord Jesus. May His name be respected, not with the lips, but with a life that is under His name, that

His name may not be put to shame because of us; rather, that His name will be glorified, will be magnified. Kingdom speaks of the sovereign rule of God. If we are called by His name, if we put ourselves under His name, then surely, His sovereign rule is over us. We become His kingdom. And His will, no doubt, is being done upon earth, in us, as it is in heaven.

The prayer that our Lord Jesus teaches us to pray is to begin with God's name, God's kingdom, and God's will. Oftentimes, we find that our prayer is rather self-centered, and does not go beyond our immediate family. We are more interested in our interests, concerned with our concerns; but the Lord Jesus wants to bring us to the right order, that we should be concerned, first, with God's concern. We should be interested in God's interests. We should not always just be concerned with ourselves, with our own welfare, and with our own interests. We need to be delivered that we might be interested in God's interests and concerned with God's concern; and that is His name, His kingdom, His will.

But seek ye first the kingdom of God and His righteousness. (Matthew 6:33)

When we are praying for His name, for His kingdom, and for His will, it may sound a little bit objective, as something outside of us; but we are very much involved in that prayer, because when we are praying for His name to be hallowed, it is to be hallowed by us. When we are praying for His kingdom to come, it is to come upon us. When we are praying for His will to be done on earth as it is in heaven, it is to be done among us and in us. We are very much involved when we are praying that kind of prayer. It does not mean that we are standing far away, praying that prayer, and God will answer it outside of us. No; God will answer that prayer within us and among us. We are very much involved in that prayer. May I put it another way? If you do not want His kingdom to come, then do not pray that prayer; because if you start to pray that prayer and God answers you, you will get into trouble.

DAILY BREAD

After we pray, "Thy name, Thy kingdom, and Thy will", then the Lord tells us to pray, "Give us this day our daily bread." This is for our physical need. God created us with a spirit, soul, and body. Our body has a need, which is daily bread; and we can pray for that. We are not commanded to pray for tomorrow's bread, but we are asked to pray for today's bread. God knows our daily needs, and we depend upon Him to supply us with our physical needs."Give us this day our daily bread."

FORGIVENESS

"Forgive us our debts, trespasses, as we forgive our debtors." This is for our psychological need or our soulical need. If we have an unforgiving spirit, then our soul is in trouble. We need to forgive our debtors because God has forgiven us so much; and who are we to hold anything against anybody? If we forgive, He will forgive us, and our soul will be healthy and sound. We will be in peace and rest. God knows that we need this; we need to pray that prayer.

Oftentimes, there is an unforgiving spirit among God's people. If unbelievers should do something against us, it is easy for us to forgive them, because, after all, they are in darkness. But if a brother or a sister should offend us, it is very hard to forgive, because we think they should know better, especially some big brothers and big sisters. But if we hold on to that bitterness, that unforgiveness, the one who suffers the most is ourselves. Our soul is sick, unhealthy, unsound, restless. This prayer needs to be prayed every day, that God will keep our soul in peace, that we know we have no controversy against anybody, that we know God does not have any controversy with us, and He is not holding anything against us.

DELIVERANCE FROM THE EVIL ONE

"Lead us not into temptation but deliver us from the evil one." We are created with a spirit, and our spirit has needs, also. The need of the spirit is that we will not enter into temptation. Now, it is true, as long as we are in the flesh, temptation seems to be unavoidable. But thank God, there are many temptations that can be avoided. Oftentimes, we try to draw temptations upon ourselves; we jump into temptations. Many temptations are unnecessary; and because we are not careful, we find ourselves being tempted all around. We need to ask the Lord, "Lead us not into temptation." We know our frailty, yet sometimes we feel we are so strong, we are so spiritual, that we can do anything. So we dare the devil to tempt us. If you are doing that, do not think that God will always protect you. Sometimes, He will; but not always. We need to know our weakness. We need to be humble before God, knowing that we are frail, and ask the Lord, "Lead us not into temptation." We are afraid that if we fall into temptation, we may yield to it and sin. In a sense, temptation, itself, is not a sin. If you are tempted, that is not a sin; but if you yield to temptation, that is sin.

Knowing ourselves, we ask the Lord, "Lead us not into temptation." But, if the Lord should see that we need to be tested, that we need to be tried, and He allows temptation to come upon us, then we ask the Lord, "Deliver us from the evil one"; because it is the evil one who is behind every temptation, and his purpose is evil. He wants to draw us away from God to fall into sin and away from the kingdom of God into the kingdom of darkness. Brothers and sisters, I do not know about you, but I do feel very strongly in myself that I should pray this prayer, daily: "Lead me not into temptation but deliver me from the evil one. For thine is the kingdom and the power and the glory forever. Amen."

Why do we pray in such a way? It is because "Thine is the kingdom. The kingdom belongs to Thee." We want to see God rule over our lives. "Thine is the power. You have the power to bring it about; and You have the glory. Everything goes back to You. Amen." So be it. This is the Lord's Prayer, the prayer of the church; and in this vein, we are to pray.

THE TWO KINGDOMS

Why do we need to pray, "Thy kingdom come"? Won't the kingdom of God just come, automatically? Does God have a timetable, and when the time comes, the kingdom comes? Why do we need to pray this prayer: "Thy kingdom come"? One reason is there are two kingdoms, now, on earth; and these two kingdoms are opposite to each other. These two kingdoms are not only outside of us, but these two kingdoms are, actually, within us. We have mentioned before that the kingdom is not just a domain, a territory, a sphere, which gives us an idea of something external, but basically, the kingdom is something internal. The kingdom is according to a nature. God's kingdom is the manifestation, the expression, the rule of His nature. In other words, if the kingdom is a matter of the Person, His personality characterizing His kingdom, His character being put upon the domain that He rules, then the kingdom is more than something external; it is something internal.

Brothers and sisters, there are two kingdoms opposite to each other, because they are of entirely opposing natures. The kingdom of God is according to the nature of God. The kingdom of Satan is according to the nature of Satan. These two kingdoms both exist on this earth, and yet, they cannot coexist. It is a contradiction. They are both here, yet they do not coexist. If this kingdom comes, then that kingdom goes. This is not only externally true, but it is inwardly real. These two opposite kingdoms are striving against each other for ascendancy within us. Who is to rule? Which kingdom will be there? Within our very being, these kingdoms are battling against each other. The spiritual conflict, the spiritual warfare is within us. These two kingdoms are fighting against each other because they cannot coexist. Therefore, we need to pray, "Thy kingdom come."

Before we knew the Lord Jesus, before we were saved, we belonged to the Satanic kingdom; we were under the power of darkness. We were under the rule of Satan, and he ruled us according to his nature. His motive is to destroy us. But thank God, one day we were saved by our Lord Jesus. "He has delivered us out of the power of darkness and has translated us into the kingdom of the Son of His love" (Colossians 1:13). So outwardly speaking, we, who believe in the Lord Jesus, have been delivered out of the kingdom of Satan. We no longer belong to him, but were translated into the kingdom of the Son of God's love. Thank God, brothers and sisters, we are now in the kingdom of God. But unfortunately, even though positionally, we are out of the power of darkness and into the kingdom of God's Son, yet, internally speaking, these two kingdoms exist within us.

Let me use an illustration. When God delivered the children of Israel out of Egypt, they crossed the Red Sea, and they were out of Egypt. They were delivered from Pharaoh and his rule. When they were under the rule of Pharaoh in Egypt, they were not allowed even to live. They were put into hard labor. All the male children were to be drowned. The purpose of Pharaoh was to annihilate them, kill them off. But thank God, He sent Moses to deliver them out of Egypt, and after they crossed the Red Sea, Egypt was behind them. In 1 Corinthians 10, it says they were baptized unto Moses, which means they were no longer under Pharaoh. They were under Moses, and Moses as representing God. They belonged to the kingdom of God now. In Exodus 15, they sang the song of victory: "Jehovah reigns forever and forever."

However, as they traveled through the wilderness, whenever they had a problem, their minds would go back to Egypt. They thought of the garlic, of the onions, and of the fishes of

Egypt, all those smelly things. Every time something happened, their minds went back to Egypt. In other words, they were delivered out of Egypt, physically, but soulically, Egypt was in them. Physically, they were out of Egypt, but spiritually, morally speaking, Egypt was still within them; Egypt was still trying to hold them. It was not until they crossed the River Jordan and God said, "The reproach of Egypt has rolled away from you" (Joshua 5:9), that they were delivered, not only outwardly, but inwardly, from Egypt. It was only then they were out of Egypt, and Egypt was out of them.

Brothers and sisters, this is a type, and it tells us our situation. In one sense, we have been delivered out of the power of darkness. We do not belong to the kingdom of God's enemy. Thank God, we are in the kingdom of God. He has translated us into that kingdom. But on the other hand, because this is a moral, spiritual thing and not a physical thing, there are two natures within us, and these two natures represent two kingdoms. They are fighting against each other within us, day after day, night after night. It is the will of God that the kingdom of darkness will be completely destroyed. God has exalted our Lord Jesus on the throne, and He is waiting for all His enemies to be His footstool. The kingdom of darkness will be completely destroyed and dismissed from our lives, and the kingdom of God shall be fully established within us. The Lordship of Christ shall be unchallenged. This is the will of God.

SATANIC KINGDOM RULED BY SIN

We say kingdom is according to nature. In other words, the Satanic kingdom is ruled by its nature, and the nature of Satan is sin. That is the reason why when Adam fell, sin entered into the world by one man. In Romans 7, it says: "Sin dwells in me, that is in my flesh." Sin is not only an act or many acts, sin is a nature of a certain kind of life. It is a power. It reigns and rules within us, that is, in our flesh. So the kingdom of darkness is not just something external. When Adam committed sin, when he betrayed the trust of God, he handed himself, and the whole earth that had been given to him, over to Satan, the enemy of God. Satan took hold of man and the earth, and he organized it into what, today, we call "the world", "the system", "the cosmos". He is the prince of this world. He organized it according to his character, his nature, and he rules it according to his character. There is that organized world which is the kingdom of Satan. He is the ruler of this world.

But brothers and sisters, it is more than that. When Adam fell and sinned, not only did he hand himself and the whole earth over to the enemy to be organized as a kingdom against God's kingdom, but sin entered into him. It dwelt in him; it ruled from within him. So the kingdom of the enemy was not only around him, but it was also within him. This was even worse than what was outside of him.

One brother says, "We want to attack the kingdom of Satan." But how do you attack it? Well, maybe you can go to China and convert the heathens. Maybe you can go to the slums in the city and try to snatch people away from the enemy. Maybe you try to attack him and his organization. But if Satan is not dethroned in your life, it is no use, because he rules by his nature. Unless that nature is dealt with, then you find his kingdom is still there. You may attack him here and attack him there, thinking that you are making some inroads, but if that nature is not dealt with, he still holds the reins. The nature of Satan is sin.

ORIGINAL SIN

Theologically, people talk about original sin. We say we have not only sinned, and that we commit many sins, but within us there is an original sin. Everybody is born with original sin. This original sin dwells in you, it rules over you, and it makes you do things that, maybe, you do not want to do or you know you should not do. It keeps you from doing things that you feel you should do; but you are helpless because there is that original sin there. The Scripture says you are a sinner before you sin. You sin because you are a sinner. Adam was an exception. He sinned, and he became a sinner. Sin dwelt in him, and he could do nothing but sin. But, we, who are born of Adam, are born with that original sin in us; and therefore, we cannot help but sin. We belong to the kingdom of Satan; we are ruled by his nature.

I used to think original sin began with Adam, but brother Sparks corrected me. Original sin did not originate with Adam. It goes way back to the archangel. There was no sin in the whole universe that God created. In the beginning, the kingdom of God was so blessed, so glorious, because everything was created according to God's nature, and every created being submitted to God's authority. God's authority was unchallenged, and He ruled over all with His benevolent rule, the blessing of the universe. You just cannot imagine. But one day, that archangel began to be interested in himself. In the beginning, in that blessed state of the kingdom of God, nobody thought of himself. Everybody thought of God. All eyes were upon God. No one tried to look within himself. But then, that archangel began to turn upon himself: "I, I, I. How about me"?" Sin begins with "I".

Pride

The seat of sin is the will. When you begin to turn upon the "I", then, the "I" wills. "I will ascend to the heavens. I will exalt my throne above the stars of God. I will join in that divine council of God in the recesses of the north. I will be above the clouds of the heavens. I will be equal with God." This is how sin began. Sin began with "I"; self; self-consciousness; self-interest; self-seeking; self-ambition; self-centeredness. That is what sin is. And the will began to exercise itself: "I want this; I want that; this is what I deserve to have; this is what I ought to be." Instead of seeing God and submitting to God, being happy with the place that God had put him, the archangel began to oppose God. He tried to set himself up. Pride is the essence of sin.

That is the reason why, in the Scriptures there are many, many strong words against the spirit of pride. God hates the proud; it is an abomination to Him. That archangel began to be proud of himself, because God had endowed him with such wisdom, God had given him such talents, God had put in his hand so much dominion, and God had set him up as an anointed, covering cherub. He was so clever, he began to be proud of himself. "I deserve something more than God has put me in. Why am I not equal with God? Why should I be under

Him?" It resulted in rebellion and perversity. That is the nature of Satan. That is original sin. Original sin is a nature; and that nature is "I", me, self, self-will, pride, myself. Have we not experienced that there is this other kingdom in us?

A NEW NATURE

After we are saved, we have the life of Christ in us. A new nature has come into us, and this new nature is to rule and to reign so that we may be in the kingdom of God. Whenever we allow that nature to develop and follow that nature, there is peace, there is joy, there is rest, there is blessedness. It is the kingdom of God. "There is righteousness and peace and joy in the Holy Spirit." Is it not true in our personal experience? But, unfortunately, there is another nature within us. Sin tries to raise its head, again and again. It tries to fight against God's kingdom within us, to snatch us away from God's kingdom and put us under his rule. The "I" comes in; self raises its head; and pride follows. When we are in that kind of situation, we sense death within us. The two kingdoms are within us. Is there any salvation? Thank God, there is!

CHRIST IS THE KINGDOM OF GOD

One day, God's Son came into this world to be a Man. In that Man, there is no original sin. That is the reason why He must be born of a virgin, because He is born of the Spirit. The Holy Spirit overshadowed the womb of that virgin, Mary, and she gave birth to the Holy One. We all are born with original sin. The kingdom of darkness is within us. But here is a Man who was born the Holy One; there is no original sin there.

If you read the life of our Lord Jesus, you find His whole life is the kingdom of God. He not only came as the King of the Jews, but He, Himself, is the kingdom of God. In His life, God is all and in all. The personal rule of God is evident in His whole life. Never once did He rebel against God; never once did He think of Himself. He denied Himself; He did the will of God; He is the kingdom of God.

Temptations Of Christ

But do you think that He did not go through the battle of the two kingdoms? He did; although not within Him, but outside of Him. After He was born, the kingdom of darkness was so aroused, they knew the kingdom of God had finally come upon this earth; and one day, that kingdom would destroy the kingdom of darkness. You remember, almost immediately after our Lord Jesus was born, Herod wanted to kill Him, and He had to flee to Egypt. It was Satan behind Herod.

When He began to come forth at the age of thirty, He went to be baptized; and after His baptism, the Holy Spirit drove Him to the wilderness to meet His enemy. There, Satan tempted Him with everything that he could do. There is no temptation that anybody in this whole world can ever be tempted with that our Lord Jesus was not tempted with. In other words, Satan exhausted all his tactics upon our Lord Jesus, trying to break into the kingdom of God, trying to break Him and put Him under his kingdom. "You are hungry. If you are the Son of

God, make the stones bread and eat it. You can do it." But our Lord Jesus said:

Man shall not live by bread alone, but by every word which goes out through God's mouth. (Matthew 4:4)

This is the kingdom of God in His life. Satan took Him to the pinnacle of the temple and said: "You are born a King. You are going to have Your kingdom. You jump down. Everybody will see someone descending out of heaven, and they will worship You, and they will follow You. You will have Your kingdom right away; this is a short cut." But our Lord Jesus said:

Thou shalt not tempt the Lord thy God. (Matthew 4:7)

God has His time, God has His way. You have to do it His way. Then Satan took Him to a high mountain and showed Him all the kingdoms of the world and all his glory, and Satan said: "It is all mine. If You bow before me, I will give it to You. It is Yours." And the Lord Jesus said:

Thou shalt do homage to the Lord thy God, and him alone shalt thou serve. (Matthew 4:10)

Satan offered his kingdom to our Lord Jesus, but our Lord Jesus repudiated it. The Lord said: "No; this is not the kingdom I want. This is another kingdom. I came to establish the kingdom of God." Yet, throughout His life, again and again, He was challenged and tempted by the external kingdom, by the kingdom of this world. "You can have it; You can have it now." But the Lord Jesus said: "No; one day, I will have it. The kingdom of the world will become the kingdom of My God and of His Christ (Revelation 11:15). But not in this way." It has to start from within. It has to be transformed. It is not easy to reject the world when it is within your reach. Because of this, He was crucified.

THE KINGDOM OF DARKNESS DESTROYED

Brothers and sisters, in our Lord Jesus' life, you see the kingdom of God, and you see the kingdom of God in ascendancy. The kingdom of darkness was destroyed. The very life of our Lord Jesus on earth has destroyed the kingdom of darkness. Our Lord Jesus said: "The prince of this world has come but he has no part in Me, no place in Me" (John 14:30). The kingdom of darkness tried to find a foothold into His life, but there was no ground for him. He defeated Satan by undercutting his ground.

And the Lord Jesus said: "For judgment, because the prince of this world is judged" (John 16:11). How does the Lord Jesus judge the prince of this world? First, morally, and spiritually, He defeats his ground. He takes away his ground, and that is how he is judged. Eventually, of course, he will be cast into the lake of fire; but it is spiritual first, and then physical. I often think, so far as the Lord is concerned, that is enough. The kingdom of God has come in that Person, and has defeated the kingdom of Satan; but for our sakes, He went to the cross. There, on the cross, He defeated the kingdom of Satan, for our sake. His life has already overcome; but there, on the cross, He undercut that ground for us that we may be delivered completely from the power of darkness, and we, too, may overcome.

Our old man has been crucified with him, (Christ) that the body of sin might be annulled, that we should no longer serve sin. (Romans 6:6)

We have that original sin within us, dwelling in the old man. That is his domain. Our Lord Jesus took that old man with Him and crucified him on the cross. He isolated that sin so that it could not reach the body anymore and command the body to sin; so the body is out of sin's employment. If you see this, then you will sing with Paul:

I am crucified with Christ, and no longer live, I, but Christ lives in me; but in that I now live in flesh, I live by faith, the faith of the Son of God, who has loved me and given himself for me. (Galatians 2:20)

"I"; the very nature of sin, "I" have been crucified with Christ. That blown-up "I" was crucified; what is left is the "I" that God has created. It is Christ who lives in me. It is the kingdom of God. We need to have our eyes opened by the Spirit of God; we need revelation. We need to see that when Christ died on the cross, we died. The "I" was crucified. It is no longer "I". The ground that Satan had to work is being removed. It is Christ who lives in me.

THE WORK OF THE HOLY SPIRIT

If sin is the principle of the kingdom of Satan, then the Spirit of God is the principle of the kingdom of God. God put His own Spirit in us. The Holy Spirit now dwells in our spirit. He is God's nature; He is life. He is in charge of the kingdom of God in us. That is the reason why we need to obey the Holy Spirit. The Holy Spirit teaches us in all things. The Holy Spirit glorifies Christ. The Holy Spirit leads us into all truth. The Holy Spirit develops that new nature within us into the character of Christ. The Holy Spirit will convict us whenever self tries to raise its head. Whenever "I" begins to come, the Holy Spirit will remind us and deliver it unto death. We need to cooperate with the Holy Spirit; and as we follow the Holy Spirit and walk after the Spirit, the kingdom of darkness subsides and disappears, and the kingdom of God rises up in glory; it is something within us. And of course, we know the church is that corporate expression of the kingdom of God.

Shall we pray:

Dear Heavenly Father, how we praise and thank Thee that Thou did send Thy beloved Son to come to deliver us who were stuck in a hopeless, helpless state. Thou does not only deliver us out of the world and translate us into Thy kingdom, but we praise and thank Thee Thou has put Thy kingdom within us. Oh, we just ask that Thy Holy Spirit will so take charge over us to build that kingdom within us that we may see Thy glory. Lord, our prayer is: "Thy kingdom come." In Thy precious name. Amen.

THE SAINTS SHALL POSSESS

Luke 12:32 Fear not, little flock, for it has been the good pleasure of your Father to give you the kingdom.

Daniel 7:13-18 I saw in the night visions, and behold, there came with the clouds of heaven one like a son of man, and he came up even to the Ancient of days, and they brought him near before him. And there was given him dominion, and glory, and a kingdom, that all peoples, nations, and languages should serve him: his dominion is an everlasting dominion, which shall not pass away, and his kingdom that which shall not be destroyed. As for me Daniel, my spirit was grieved in the midst of my body, and the visions of my head troubled me. I came near unto one of them that stood by, and asked him the certainty of all this. And he told me, and made me know the interpretation of the things: These great beasts, which are four, are four kings, that shall arise out of the earth. But the saints of the most high places shall receive the kingdom, and they shall possess the kingdom forever, even to the ages of ages.

Matthew 24:14 And these glad tidings of the kingdom shall be preached in the whole habitable earth, for a witness to all the nations, and then shall come the end.

Matthew 28:18-20 And Jesus coming up spoke to them, saying, All power has been given me in heaven and upon earth. Go therefore and make disciples of all the nations, baptising them to the name of the Father, and of the Son, and of the Holy Spirit; teaching them to observe all things whatsoever I have enjoined you. And behold, I am with you all the days, until the completion of the age.

Shall we pray:

Dear Heavenly Father, as we gather together for this time, we want to give thanks unto Thee. Thou has been good to us. We praise and thank Thee that Thou has gathered us from all places that we may meet together before Thee in the name of Thy Son, our Lord Jesus. We do praise and thank Thee for Thy presence with us and for Thy blessing upon us. So Father, we just want to bow down and worship Thee, that our God is really good. Oh, how we praise and thank Thee that Thou does promise us that goodness and mercy shall follow us all the days of our lives. We just come again this morning, committing this time into Thy hands. We pray that, by Thy Spirit, Thou will sum up all things and bring us to a higher plane that we may walk forward and onward towards the goal. We trust Thy Holy Spirit to illumine Thy Word, to make Thy Word living to us, life and spirit to us Lord. Without Thy speaking, everything will be in vain, but we thank and praise Thee that with Thy speaking to our heart, Thou art able to accomplish Thy purpose. So, we just commit this time into Thy hands and trust Thee for it, and to Thee be the glory. In the name of our Lord Jesus. Amen.

We believe that the kingdom of God is very much upon the heart of God. It was conceived in God's heart even before He began creation. It was with the kingdom in view that He created the universe. He created all things according to His character, and then He ruled over all things according to His character. This is the kingdom of God. Even though there were rebellions, not only among the angelic beings but also in man, nevertheless, "The heavens do rule." The Lord teaches His people to pray. We, who are redeemed by the precious blood, who have been delivered out of the power of darkness and translated into the kingdom of the Son of God's love, are to pray, "Thy kingdom come." As we pray, "Thy kingdom come", it is not with the idea that we are praying for the coming of the kingdom in the distant future; but He wants that kingdom to come now and here, in us and among us. We are very much involved in this kingdom.

As we conclude this subject, I have to say that the kingdom is such a tremendous theme in the Word of God that we cannot finish it in four sessions. As a matter of fact, we are just touching it very lightly, and I do believe that there is much, much more that the Spirit of God will teach us in the days to come. So I pray the Lord will continue to search our hearts and stir our spirits, and continue to reveal His kingdom to us that, more and more, His kingdom may be in us. How much we are in the kingdom of God depends on how much the kingdom is within us.

May our lives upon this earth be such that we really hasten the coming of that kingdom upon this earth. So we would like to share together on this matter of the saints possessing the kingdom.

SEEK THE KINGDOM

Seek ye first the kingdom of God and his righteousness and all these things shall be added unto you. (Matthew 6:33)

The word seek is very special. After we have heard or seen something of the meaning of the kingdom of God, something of the nature of that kingdom, then we are exhorted to seek after it. We cannot just hear about it, and then forget it altogether. We have to apply ourselves in diligently searching and seeking after it. The very word seek implies putting our heart into it. It means that we are determined to pay any cost to get it. We will not be turned aside or turned away from it until we find it. "Seek and ye shall find." So, we are exhorted by our Lord, Himself, to seek the kingdom of God and His righteousness.

However, we are living in a very hostile world. Even though the Lord has delivered us out of the power of darkness and has translated us into the kingdom of the Son of God's love, yet, we are still living in this world. We are living in a world in which the prince, the ruler of this world, is the enemy of God. He is trying every way to compromise us, to pressure us and to destroy us. The cares of this world, what we shall eat, what we shall drink, what we shall be clothed with, are very real to us. They are pressing upon us, trying to take our time away from God, trying to take our energy away from God, and even trying to take our heart away from God. Everything around us seems to be trying to take us out of the kingdom of God and draw us back into the kingdom of Satan. We are under great pressure. More than that, not only do we have enemies all around us, but the enemy is even within us. The battle is going on within us: the kingdom of God against the kingdom of darkness, the kingdom of darkness against the kingdom of God. Sometimes, the battle is so fierce we wonder whether we will survive.

THE FATHER HAS GIVEN US THE KINGDOM

How can we seek the kingdom of God and His righteousness? Thank God, after our Lord Jesus exhorted us to seek the kingdom of God and His righteousness, He said:

Fear not little flock, it has been the good pleasure of the Father to give you the kingdom. (Luke 12:32)

When we see the kingdom of God and we realize what the kingdom is and how important it is to God and to us, don't we begin to be afraid? We are apprehensive as to whether this kingdom of God will be a reality in our lives, whether we will be in God's hands to bring in His kingdom. We find that we are so weak and so fragile that we tend to fall. How can we fulfill that mission that God has entrusted to us, individually, and as the church? But the Lord Jesus said: "Fear not, little flock." Actually, "little flock" is just another name for the church; because so far as the people of God are concerned, we are like a little flock in comparison with the population of the world. The world is full of people; yet God has taken some people out of every nation, every tribe, every tongue, and every people and brought them together under the name of the Lord Jesus. This people is just a little flock; and we live among wolves. How can we survive? How can we stand as witnesses to the kingdom of God? How can we maintain the testimony of the kingdom? "Fear not, little flock, for it has been the good pleasure of your Father to give you the kingdom."

Brothers and sisters, in one sense, we have to seek, we have to fight, we have to win the kingdom; but, in another sense, the Father has already given it to us, and it is the good pleasure of the Father to give us the kingdom. A good father always gives the best to his children. It is the will, it is the delight of our Heavenly Father to give us the kingdom. He sent His Son into this world to recapture that kingdom for us, and He put His Holy Spirit in us to bring us into all the realities of the kingdom. God is working for us; and if God is for us, who can stand against us? "Fear not, little flock, it has been the good pleasure of the Father to give you the kingdom."

DANIEL THE PROPHET OF THE KINGDOM

Daniel is the prophet of the kingdom. Most likely, he came from a royal family of Judah, but he was taken as a captive in his young years and brought into Babylon. There, in the sovereignty of God, he became the governor of the greatest empire of the world at that time. His whole life was connected with government, with dominion, and with kingdom.

Daniel, chapters 1-6, speak of his public history. He was determined not to be polluted; he wanted to keep himself pure for God. The kingdom of God was upon him, even though Israel, as a nation, had failed. The government of this earth had passed into the hands of the Gentiles; yet, in that one man, the kingdom of God still existed; in that one man, the heavens still ruled; in that one man, the personal rule of God was most evident. He determined to keep himself pure for God; and God kept him, God blessed him, and God used him to be a witness and a testimony of the kingdom of God in the midst of the kingdom of the world.

THE VISION

Daniel began in the days of Nebuchadnezzar, king of Babylon. He continued on through the days of Darius, the Medo-Persian king, and even to the reign of Cyrus. Chapters 7-12 of Daniel are the private history of Daniel; and in chapter 7, he saw night visions. He saw the wind blowing upon the sea and four great beasts coming out of the sea; and in the last beast, he saw a little horn. Finally, he saw the throne set up, and the Ancient of Days took His place on the throne, where He began to judge the world. Then, Daniel saw one like a Son of Man. He was led to the Ancient of Days; and to Him was given a kingdom, that all peoples, all nations would come under His rule and dominion. Now, Daniel wanted to understand his vision, so he inquired and was told what it meant.

Actually, the vision that God gave to Daniel was the same dream that God gave to King Nebuchadnezzar. King Nebuchadnezzar saw a huge man, a super man. He saw a man with a golden head, with silver, brass and iron. He had a brass belly with iron legs, and feet partly of iron and partly of clay. As he looked at that immense image, suddenly, a stone, not cut out with hands, fell upon that image, smashing it until it disappeared. This stone grew and filled the whole earth. Now, that was the vision given to Nebuchadnezzar.

Daniel saw the same vision, but in a very different way. From the human standpoint, we think of the empires of this world or the governments of this world as a human image: glorious, strong, and powerful. As far as God's view is concerned, the kingdoms of this world are like wild beasts. So, to Daniel, seeing the government of this world in the hands of man during the times of the Gentiles, was like being governed by great beasts that destroyed and killed each other.

In his dream, Nebuchadnezzar saw a living stone, and in the vision given to Daniel he saw one like a Son of Man. This Son of Man is none other than our Lord Jesus Christ; and he saw that, in the end, Christ shall inherit the world, because He is worthy. When our Lord Jesus was upon this earth, He was the kingdom of God on this earth. Throughout the life of our Lord Jesus, God is all and all in Him. He repudiated this other world. He would have nothing to do with that kingdom, even though it was offered to Him. He rejected it; and because He rejected that kingdom, He was put out; He was crucified. "Away with Him." Yet, on the cross, He spoiled the principalities and authorities and He made a public show of them. His victory was complete. On the cross, our Lord Jesus took the kingdom out of the hands of the enemy. He recaptured it and gave it to His church. He has redeemed a people, and given His life to that people. The Spirit of God dwells in that people. Now, the Lord says: "You are My kingdom upon this earth."

THE CHURCH IS THE EMBODIMENT OF THE KINGDOM

On the day of Pentecost, the Holy Spirit came down upon the 120 people. These 120 people were 120 individual believers, even though, probably, they were the best. I do believe that if you had such a congregation, you would feel so happy. You would think, "Well, what else can you have?" But God is not satisfied with that. The Holy Spirit came down upon the 120; and in one Spirit they were baptized into one body, one body of 120 members. And it is to that body Christ entrusted His kingdom. He said: "You are My kingdom. Go out and preach the good tidings of the kingdom of God."

What is the church? The church is the embodiment of the kingdom of God on earth, today.

For where two or three are gathered together unto my name, there am I in the midst of them. (Matthew 18:20)

Two or three is the minimum of plurality. The church is where two or three are gathered together, assembled together, and where, they are not each going his or her own way, as individual believers. If we stand as individual believers, all scattered, then the enemy is able to pick us off, one by one; we do not have the strength to resist the kingdom of darkness and to usher in the kingdom of God. So it is the will of God to assemble us together unto "My name", in the name of the Lord Jesus. Do you know what that means? We, who call upon that name, put ourselves under the authority of that name; we take His name upon us. Our names are nothing, but His name becomes everything.

In a wedding, when a woman is married to a man, it is the custom, from that day onward, that she drop her family name and take up the family name of her husband. It means, from now on, the head of the family is who the name is. When we gather together unto the name of the Lord Jesus, we drop our name, we lay down our rights, we lay down our authority, we take Him as our Head, and we submit ourselves to His ruler-ship. The Lord says: "I am in the midst of you." The Pharisees asked the Lord: "When will the kingdom of God come? How does it come? Where?" And the Lord said: "The kingdom of God does not come by observation. You cannot say here or there; but the kingdom of God is in the midst of you" (Luke 17:20-21).

Dear brothers and sisters, what is the church? The church is a people assembled unto the name of the Lord Jesus. The church is a body submitted to and joined to the Head, and holding fast the Head. And if this is what the church is, then this is, also, what the kingdom of God is. So, in spiritual reality, the church, today, is the kingdom of God on earth. Unfortunately, this does not seem to be true. God's people are scattered: picked-up, picked-out, picked-off, one by one. God's people are not assembled under that name. The Lordship of Christ is overlooked, man begins to rule, and the testimony of the kingdom of God suffers. The church is the embodiment of the kingdom of God.

EVIDENCES OF THE RISEN CHRIST

The Holy Spirit Came Down

In the book of Daniel, the Son of Man came, and a kingdom was given to Him. It is because of the finished work of Christ: His victory in His life, in His death on the cross, and His resurrection. Revelation 5, actually gives us a review of the ascension of our Lord Jesus. No one has ever seen what happened when the Lord ascended and arrived in heaven. The disciples saw Him going up from the Mount of Olives and being taken away by a cloud. They could not see Him anymore. They wondered whether He arrived or not. Where is the assurance that our Lord Jesus arrived in heaven? How do we know that God did not cast Him off in some valley as the sons of the prophets told Elisha? (see 2 Kings 2:16).

We know our Lord Jesus arrived in heaven because, on the day of Pentecost, the Holy Spirit was given. As our Lord Jesus ascended to the throne, God anointed Him as Lord and King; and this anointing was manifested, was proven, was evidenced by the outpouring of the Holy Spirit on the day of Pentecost. In Psalm 133, it says: "The holy ointment was poured upon the head of Aaron. It flowed down to his beard, and it continued to flow and fill unto the skirt of his garment." When the Head was anointed, the Holy Spirit came down, and the anointing covered the whole body. That was the experience of the day of Pentecost.

The Kingdom Recaptured

However, there is further evidence of the Lord Jesus' arrival in heaven. When John was on the Island of Patmos, God gave him a vision. He was taken to heaven, and he saw a Lamb, newly slain. This Lamb came and took that little book from the hand of the One who sits upon the throne. After He took that little book, there was worship, praise, honor, adoration, and singing of songs of the Redeemer and His redeemed. He began to open the book, for He, alone, is worthy. I feel that Revelation 4 is a review of the glory of the Creator, and Revelation 5 is a review of the glory of the Redeemer.

Our Lord Jesus ascended upon high as a Lamb, newly slain. But because of His finished work on the cross, He has overcome the kingdom of darkness; He has bound the strong man; He has spoiled him; He has taken out the captives and set them free. He is worthy to take the world in His hand, to recapture the kingdom for God; and that is what He did. He took the book, the title deed of the universe. God never gave up His ownership, even though there was that usurper, a squatter on earth. You know, when you have people squatting on your territory or on your property, it is very hard to get rid of them because they think they own it. Then, you really need some authority and power to cast them out.

But, who has the authority? Man has fallen into the hands of the enemy. There is no one in heaven, on earth, underneath the earth; no one is worthy; no one has the right; no one has the authority; no one has the power. No doubt John wept because he thought, "Now we are finished. Now the world is finished. There is no more hope. The kingdom of God was dismissed to heaven; it can never appear on earth."

Thank God, there is ONE. He has overcome; He is worthy; He has the authority; He has the right to take the kingdom in His hand; He has the power to bring it back to Him. Then, there is the opening of the seals. Even though the enemy tries to oppose it and tries to stir up all kinds of plagues, wars, rumors of wars, shedding of blood, famine, pestilence and all these woes upon this earth, yet, out of it, something is born. God is bringing back His kingdom to man.

I am really touched by Daniel 7, which says that one like the Son of Man came, and He was given a kingdom because He is worthy. But when the angel began to explain it to Daniel, he said: "The saints of the most high places shall possess the kingdom and they shall reign forever." The kingdom is given to Christ; but we shall possess the kingdom. You can never separate the head and the body. The kingdom is given to the Head, and He has every right to have it, because He has recaptured it; but after He has recaptured it, He gives it to His body: "the saints of the most high places". I believe that refers to the church, because we are seated with Him in the heavenlies, and the kingdom is ours. We are heirs of God and coheirs of Christ. "The saints of the most high places shall possess the kingdom."

On the one hand, it is all the work of our Lord Jesus; if He had not recaptured it, we would never possess it. But, on the other hand, the kingdom is a spiritual thing, a moral thing; it is not just an external, outward thing. So, even though our Lord Jesus has recaptured the kingdom and given it to us, we have to let the character of that One characterize us for us to really possess it.

THE TESTIMONY OF THE EARLY CHURCH

Let's look into the book of Acts. I believe every believer loves to read the first four

119

chapters of the book of Acts because it tells us of the beginning of the church. On the day of Pentecost, the Holy Spirit came down and the 120 people were baptized into one body. Immediately, they began to declare, to proclaim the kingdom of God. Peter stood up, and the eleven stood up with him. There was no more jealousy and no more striving: "Who is greater?" They were of one heart, one mind, one soul, one spirit, and one body. The first gospel message of the body of Christ is the message of the kingdom: "What you have heard and seen is this, God has raised Jesus from the dead. The One who was crucified, God has made Him Lord and Christ" (see Acts 2:32,36). On the day of Pentecost, the kingdom of God became a reality in the lives of the 120 people. They not only proclaimed it, they lived it. Because of that, the power of the kingdom of God was manifested and 3000 came in. Very soon, 4000 more came in.

This people, whom God had set apart for Himself, persevered in the teaching and fellowship of the apostles, in the breaking of bread, and prayer. They continued on in the teaching of the apostles. The teaching of the apostles is nothing but the teaching of Christ. They continued on in the fellowship of the apostles. The fellowship of the apostles is the fellowship of the Son and of the Father.

That which we have seen and heard we reported to you, that ye also may have fellowship with us; and our fellowship is indeed with the Father and with His Son Jesus Christ. (1 John 1:3)

They continued on breaking bread, not once a year, not once a month, not once a week; but, in the early days, they broke bread every day. Some people say, "This is Saturday; why should we break bread? This is not Sunday." In the early church, they broke bread from house to house, daily, because they loved the Lord. They wanted to remember Him. Their hearts were captured by Him. They wanted to worship Him and praise Him. At that time, God had delivered them completely out of self. The ground of the kingdom of darkness had really been undercut among this people. Nobody thought of himself. People who had property and saw all the other brothers and sisters in need sold their property and laid it at the feet of the apostles to be distributed to all who were in need. There was no more self.

Self-possessiveness is one of the strongest instincts in man. We want to possess for ourselves. Even children, when they are playing with their toys, will snatch a toy out of the hand of a friend and say, "This is mine." Self-possessiveness is a strong instinct. But in the early church, that self, the ground upon which the kingdom of darkness is built, was completely uprooted. There was no self; it was Christ.

Oh, how they loved one another! The testimony of the early church was people looking at them and saying, "See how they love one another." They were the kingdom of God, and they lived the kingdom of God. Therefore, when they proclaimed it, it had power and authority.

When the kingdom is proclaimed, without doubt it is a challenge. You either accept it or you reject it. If you accept it, then you capitulate to Christ. It is not just a matter of taking Christ as your Saviour, that you may go to heaven and not to hell; it is a matter of taking Christ as your

Lord, as your King, and as your Master. You allow Him to rule over your life; you allow the Holy Spirit to incorporate, to develop, to form Christ in you; and, as a people, you put yourself under the Headship of Christ. You let Christ be the Head and let His rule be unchallenged. You are the embodiment of the kingdom of God.

However, when the kingdom is preached, you may reject it. It is too costly; the demand is too absolute; and you refuse to accept the Lordship of Christ. When you do that, invariably, you will begin to oppose and persecute those who believe.

The kingdom is never a neutral thing. It is either this or that. When the kingdom comes, it is a living power. It either brings people into subjection unto Christ or it stirs up opposition. You will find this in the book of Acts. As this people spread out, they took the message with them; and wherever they went, thank God, there were people who surrendered to the Lordship of Christ. But there were other people who were stirred to jealousy and who tried to kill and destroy them. It is always like that, because the kingdom of God is not a theory; it is a life. It is not a doctrine, a teaching; it is a power. When our Lord Jesus was on earth, people could not take Him; He was too hard. So they rejected Him, and killed Him. There is no middle ground.

How powerful the church was in the beginning! The church is the very embodiment of the kingdom of God. The church is a vessel in God's hand. It is an instrument in God's hand to spread the kingdom and to bring in the kingdom of God upon this earth. In spite of all opposition, the Roman Empire was destroyed, not the church.

FAILURE OF THE CHURCH

Unfortunately, what happened to Israel, happened to the church. History repeats itself. Very soon, the kingdom of darkness tried every way to infiltrate into the kingdom of God and to destroy it from within. In chapter 5 of the book of Acts, Satan seemed to fill the hearts of a couple to try to deceive the Holy Spirit. They tried to do something that looked good in order to gain a name for themselves, not in the world, but in the church. But the Holy Spirit was so present, immediately, the judgment came. The name of the Lord Jesus was exalted.

In Acts 3, Peter and John said to the lame man: "Silver and gold we have not; but what we have, we give it to you: In the name of the Lord Jesus rise up and walk." That cripple leaped up and walked, praising God. The Name, power.

Satan tried every way to infiltrate into the kingdom of God. In Acts 6, there were murmurings. But, under the wisdom of the Holy Spirit, the apostles were able to solve the problem, immediately, and actually open a new door for many more to come to the Lord.

The Word prospered. The enemy tried to use outward persecution to destroy the church, but instead, the church spread to other cities, from the city of Judea to Samaria. Philip went to Samaria where He preached the kingdom of God and the things of the Lord Jesus, and many came to the Lord. The persecuted people spread all over to Antioch, Selecia, and many other places.

Even in the days of the early apostles, the kingdom of darkness tried to make an inroad into the kingdom of God. There were false teachings, false doctrines, false prophets, false teachers, and false apostles. There were Judiazers trying to corrupt the kingdom of God and trying to change the nature of the gospel of Jesus Christ, saying that He is not all and in all, He is not supreme. They said that even salvation needs you to work: "You believe in Him, and you keep the commandments."

When it comes to the end of the first century, the Apostle John, for the Word of God and for the testimony of Jesus, was exiled into the island of Patmos. There God gave him a vision of the seven golden lampstands, the churches of Asia, with the Son of God in the midst of them. From this vision, we see that even towards the end of the first century, the reality of the Lordship of Christ had not only been challenged, but had been compromised, and even set aside in some of the churches. Man had taken the place of Christ. No wonder there is no testimony. Because of this, the Holy Spirit is calling for repentance.

Brothers and sisters, it is not a matter of outward existence. These seven churches existed in Asia at that time, and some of them even continued on. It is not a matter of outward existence, it is a matter of inward quality. Is the church the embodiment of the kingdom of God? Is Christ on the throne of the church? Is He the Head of the body? Oh, the Spirit of God calls His people to repent. "He who overcomes."

THE OVERCOMERS

Christ recaptured the kingdom and entrusted it to the church, but the church seems to have lost it again. The church of God has compromised; but thank God, He is calling, in the church, among God's people, those who have ears to hear and who will respond to Him. He is calling those who will repent and recapture that vision, that commission, that entrusting; those who are willing to pay any cost to deny themselves, to take up the cross and follow the Lord; those who are willing to be unpopular, even hated; those who will respond to the Holy Spirit, to return to the reality of the kingdom of

God. No doubt, they will become the target of the enemy.

In Daniel 7, the little horn, the antichrist, fights against the saints of the most high places. He will wear them out. He will try to bother you, and bother you, and bother you; until, finally, he wears you out. He will kill. We read that these things will happen in the last days, but the spirit of the antichrist is already here. However, in Revelation 12:10, it says: "They overcome him." "Him" refers to the accuser. "They" refers to the man-child. The man-child is born through the travail of the woman. Out of the travail of the church, a company, a remnant, overcomers are being born; and they overcome the enemy by the blood of the Lamb. The overcomers are not super-Christians; they are not perfect. The overcomers of the church are like the rest of the church, but they know the blood of the Lamb. Whenever they are convicted by the Holy Spirit, they go to the blood of the Lamb. They do not continue on in sin; they do not continue on in self; they do not continue on in the world. Whenever the Holy Spirit convicts them of something that is not of Christ, that is out of the character of Christ, they repent. They claim the blood of the Lord Jesus, and they are washed white as snow. Their communion with God is not interrupted. They do not look back; they move on.

They have overcome him (the enemy) by reason of the blood of the Lamb, and by reason of the word of their testimony. (Revelation 12:11)

They have a testimony: Jesus is Lord. And because they live it, therefore, when they say it, there is power.

They have not loved their life even unto death.

They are willing to deny themselves and follow the Lord. When the kingdom of God is formed in a people, they defeat the kingdom of darkness in their lives. Because of this, when the man-child is born, he is taken to the throne. To be taken to the throne, they have to pass through the air, which is the headquarters of the kingdom of darkness. They have overcome the enemy in their lives, so they can fly through the headquarters of the enemy and reach the throne.

When they reach the throne, Michael and his angels will be sent to fight against Satan and his followers, and there will be no more place for them in the air. Satan will be cast down upon this earth. Who will pave the way? The overcomers. They will pave the way for the coming of Christ. They paved the way for the day when Christ shall return and rule over the whole earth. It has to be real in the lives of a people, if not the whole church, then a people in the church, the overcomers, before it can become a reality upon this earth. Thank God, He is calling overcomers everywhere: those who will respond to the calling of the Spirit of God; those who will put themselves under the Lordship of Christ; those who will say, "Jesus is Lord."

PROCLAIMING THE GOSPEL OF THE KINGDOM

And these glad tidings of the kingdom shall be preached in the whole habitable earth, for a witness to all the nations, and then shall come the end. (Matthew 24:14)

The kingdom is the gospel. Sometimes, when we think of the kingdom, we are fearful, because we think it is so heavy; it is so hard, so difficult, so costly. We think it is not a glad tiding, but a woe tiding; and it is better that we do not hear it. We just want to hear the gospel of grace: God forgives me; He saves me; He allows me to go to heaven and live there forever. We do not want to hear of the gospel of the kingdom because we think it is not the gospel.

There is no blessing more blessed than when you put yourself under the Lordship of Christ. One day, when the whole earth shall be under His rule, what a blessing it will be. Even the sun will be seven times brighter than today; and you can stand it, and enjoy it. The lion will lie down with the lamb. Nothing will hurt in the whole field of God. A child can play at the serpent's hole. Peace, love, and everything that is of God's character will rule over the earth. There is no blessing more blessed than that.

The kingdom is the gospel; and this kingdom has to be preached, heralded, proclaimed, and announced. Let it be announced to all the habitable earth. Let everybody hear about it. But, of course, you cannot announce it if it is not real

131

to you. First, it must be real in you. The kingdom is in you; then, you can announce it to the world, and more will be brought into the kingdom of God. Then, the end shall come. When Christ shall put all things under His feet, then He will give all things back to God, that God may be all and in all.

We often think of the great commission: "Go ye therefore; preach the glad tidings, that people may be saved, and heaven filled; empty hell and fill heaven." No. Our Lord Jesus said:

All power has been given me in heaven and upon earth. (Matthew 28:18)

He has recaptured the kingdom of God."All power in heaven and earth has been given to me."Now go; in the authority and power of God. We go and disciple all nations. We help people to be put under the discipline of Christ that they may be under the rulership of Christ. That is the kingdom.

Baptising them to the name of the Father, and of the Son, and of the Holy Spirit. (Matthew 28:19)

Baptism is a public confession. It is an expression of our faith. God has already taken us out of the power of darkness and translated us into the kingdom of the Son of God's love. God has done it; and now, I take baptism. In other words, I respond to that and say, "Yes. God has taken me out of the power of darkness. I am out. I am buried with Christ. God has translated me into the kingdom of the Son of God's love. Yes; I step over; I come out of the water; I belong to Him."It is a step of faith. It is the beginning of a life of discipleship. It is saying, "Now, I give up myself to You. You can do anything You like with me."

Teaching them to observe all things whatsoever I have enjoined you. (Matthew 28:20)

"Teach them the kingdom. Tell them the things about Me, and I will be with you unto the ends of the ages."The church is not only the embodiment of the kingdom of God, the church is the heralder of the kingdom. We have a responsibility, not only to receive the kingdom, but to preach the kingdom, that the kingdom may extend. That stone will smash the image and will grow and become a great mountain. One day, the kingdom of this world shall become the kingdom of our God and of His Christ. May the Lord help us.

Dear Heavenly Father, we do want to praise and thank Thee, because it is all of Thy good pleasure. It is all by the finished work of Christ. It is all by the power of the Holy Spirit. Oh, our Father, give us vision. Enable us to surrender ourselves to Thee, give up our rights, and let Thee have full sway over us, not only individually, but together; that Thy kingdom may become a reality in us today, and we may be able to proclaim the gospel of Jesus Christ. In the name of our Lord Jesus. Amen.

Other Books Printed By
Christian Testimony Ministry

SPEAKER	TITLE
DANA CONGDON	MARRIAGE, SINGLENESS, AND THE WILL OF GOD
	RECOVERY & RESTORATION
	THE HOLY SPIRIT
	HEBREWS
A.J. FLACK	TENT OF HIS SPLENDOUR
STEPHEN KAUNG	ACTS
	BE YE THEREFORE PERFECT
	CALLED OUT UNTO CHRIST
	CALLED TO THE FELLOWSHIP OF GOD'S SON
	DIVINE LIFE AND ORDER
	FOR ME TO LIVE IS CHRIST
	GLORIOUS LIBERTY OF THE CHILDREN OF GOD
	GOD'S PURPOSE FOR THE FAMILY
	I WILL BUILD MY CHURCH
	MEDITATIONS ON THE KINGDOM
	RECOVERY
	SPIRITUAL EXERCISE
	SPIRITUAL LIFE (II CORINTHIANS SERIES)
	TEACH US TO PRAY
	THE CROSS
	THE FULNESS OF CHRIST—IN THE BOOK OF REVELATION
	THE HEADSHIP OF CHRIST
	THE KINGDOM AND THE CHURCH
	THE KINGDOM OF GOD
	THE LAST CALL TO THE CHURCHES, THE CALL TO OVERCOME
	THE LIFE OF OUR LORD JESUS
	THE LIFE OF THE CHURCH, THE BODY OF CHRIST
	THE LORD'S TABLE
	TWO GUIDEPOSTS FOR INHERITING THE KINGDOM
	VISION OF CHRIST (REVELATION)
	WHO ARE WE?

WHY DO WE SO GATHER?
WORSHIP

LANCE LAMBERT

CALLED UNTO HIS ETERNAL GLORY
GOD'S ETERNAL PURPOSE
IN THE DAY OF THY POWER
JACOB I HAVE LOVED
LIVING FAITH
LESSONS FROM THE LIFE OF MOSES
LOVE DIVINE
MY HOUSE SHALL BE A HOUSE OF PRAYER
PREPARATION FOR THE COMING OF THE LORD
REIGNING WITH CHRIST
SPIRITUAL CHARACTER
THE GOSPEL OF THE KINGDOM
THE IMPORTANCE OF COVERING
THE LAST DAYS AND GOD'S PRIORITIES
THE PRIZE
THE SUPREMACY OF JESUS CHRIST
THINE IS THE POWER!
THOU ART MINE

T. AUSTIN-SPARKS

THE LORD'S TESTIMONY AND THE WORLD NEED

HARVEY CEDARS CONFERENCE

STEPHEN KAUNG

HEAVENLY VISION
SPIRITUAL RESPONSIBILITY

CONGDON, HILE, KAUNG

SPIRITUAL MINISTRY
SPIRITUAL AUTHORITY
SPIRITUAL HOUSE
SPIRITUAL SUBMISSION

STEPHEN KAUNG

SPIRITUAL KNOWLEDGE
SPIRITUAL POWER
SPIRITUAL REALITY
SPIRITUAL VALUE
SPIRITUAL BLESSING
SPIRITUAL DISCERNMENT